DICTIONARY OF
DREAMS

STRATHEARN

This edition published by
STRATHEARN BOOKS LIMITED
Toronto, Canada

© 1997 Children's Leisure Products Limited,
David Dale House, New Lanark ML11 9DJ, Scotland

First published in this edition 2000, reprinted 2001

Cover photograph by John Marton,
courtesy of The Image Bank

ISBN 1 84205 022 2

Printed and bound in Europe

Contents

Introduction

Why Do We Dream?

Consciousness and unconsciousness

Although it is not known exactly why it is that we dream, in psychoanalysis it has long been recognized that the unconscious has an important role to play. However, this in itself is not terribly helpful as scientists have never been entirely certain as to where consciousness ends and unconsciousness begins. Indeed, the two frequently overlap and there can really be no clear distinction between them.

We may, perhaps, accept that to be conscious means to be awake, aware of our surroundings and in control of our actions. But this does not take into account the fact that much goes on around us in our waking state of which we are generally not aware, or only aware of on a 'less conscious' level. For instance, we may be walking along a busy street, deep in thought, and be completely unaware of the noise of the traffic all around us, until something like the blast of a car horn, or the sound of a collision, alerts us to it.

Furthermore, we do not need to concentrate all the time on moving our legs in order that we might keep on walking, nor do we generally need to concentrate hard on walking in a straight line in order that we might not veer off course and into the road.

Similarly, while we are asleep and are ostensibly 'unconscious', our brains are obviously extremely active. Although we are usually unaware of much of this activity (such as the continuing control over the function of our major organs), dreams are a manifestation of this activity and are often extremely vivid. Therefore, it would seem that the brain is capable of organizing our consciousness into several levels at all times.

The physiological manifestation of the unconscious is also a grey area. However, it is known that a structure situated in the brain stem, known as the reticular formation, acts as an activator for other parts of the brain and may play a part in defining the unconscious. All sensory pathways are linked to the reticular activating system (RAS), so that when a sense receptor is stimulated this also triggers the reticular system, 'awakening' the brain so that it is fully able to respond to messages from the senses.

Sleep

Sleep is essential for the repair of the body and for cell regeneration. People deprived of sleep for lengthy periods generally become quite unwell. However, it is a complicated process, which has been the subject of much research. Broadly speaking, the average night's sleep consists of four or five distinct stages.

1. During stage one, the sleeper begins to relax and will drift in and out of a dozing sleep from which he or she is easily awakened.
2. In stage two, the individual is asleep but can still be easily roused by minor disturbances.
3. By stage three, a state of deep relaxation is reached, and it becomes very difficult to wake the sleeper. During this stage, the eyes often move from side to side.
4. In stage four, 80 per cent of the daily output of growth hormone is released, which helps in the process of repairing body tissues.

The sleeper then proceeds in reverse through the stages, but instead of waking completely after returning to stage 1, he or she will enter a different stage (stage 5), known as REM (rapid eye movement) sleep. It is during this phase that most dreaming occurs. The whole cycle from stages 1–4 and back again takes about 90–100 minutes. During the average night's sleep the cycle will repeat itself 4 or 5 times.

REM sleep

REM sleep takes its name from the characteristic eye movements that take place during this stage. Sleepers who are wakened during this phase will report that they have been dreaming. Research has shown that during REM sleep, the body's major muscle groups seem to be paralysed. This is thought to occur in order to prevent injury or uncontrolled movement during sleep.

The length of REM sleep increases with each cycle. Therefore, the longest period of REM sleep and dreaming occurs in the last third of the night. A sleeper whose REM is disrupted will automatically try to increase the time spent in REM sleep the next night to compensate. This may indicate that REM sleep, and therefore dreaming, is essential for wellbeing. Some dreaming does take place outwith REM sleep, but it tends to be much less vivid and somewhat mundane. A sleeper who is wakened during one of these dreams may report that he or she has been 'thinking' rather than dreaming.

Getting the most from sleep

In order to dream well, it is advisable to follow a few simple rules:

1. Decide your optimum amount of sleep and stick to it as much as possible. Most adults need six and a half to eight and a half hours of sleep nightly, but some can get by on as little as five hours. A few will need as much as ten hours.

   Experiment with varying lengths of sleep. When you have decided how much you need (based on assessment of work performance, levels of irritability and plain tiredness through the day), you should aim to be in bed roughly half an hour before the period of sleep commences.

2. What you have consumed in the hours preceding sleep will directly affect the nature and quality of your dreams. If your digestion is working overtime while you sleep, your dreams may be affected. It is wise, therefore, to avoid eating wind-producing foods such as raw vegetables, or foods that have a high fat content immediately before you go to bed.

   Some stimulants, such as caffeine and alcohol, affect

the time it takes to fall asleep and the quality of sleep thereafter. Similarly, sleeping tablets seem to suppress REM sleep, which is so vital to our wellbeing.

3. Do as much as possible to eliminate noise and discomfort in the immediate sleeping environment. The immediate environment can affect your dreams; many people will have experienced dreaming that the telephone is ringing, or a fire alarm is sounding, only to find later that they have slept through the noise of the alarm; or they may have dreamt of being restrained only to wake up and find that their sheets have become so entangled that they can hardly move.

Try to adopt a relaxed routine in the hour before bedtime. If the brain is overactive as the head hits the pillow, it will take some time to drift off into a deep, untroubled sleep.

Record your dreams

It is always a good idea to keep a notebook right beside the bed if you want to record your dreams. In this way, you can make a note of your impressions the moment you wake up, before the intrusions of the day cloud or distort your memory.

When people report that they have not dreamt, it is not necessarily the case; it may be that events immediately upon waking (perhaps the alarm clock, the children careering all around, the realization that they might be late for work, etc) were so intrusive that memories of dreams were pushed out of their minds. For this reason, try, if at all possible, to train yourself to wake early, before the alarm clock's sound and before household noises disturb you. You will be more likely to be able to recall your dreams in a peaceful environment. A few pages have been provided at the back of this book on which you can begin to record your dreams.

Interpreting dreams

Our dreams can often be fantastic, terrifying and hard to comprehend because they do not seem to be contained by the rules of our everyday lives. Some of the most bizarre and disturbing distortions of reality are commonly experienced by dreamers, and the interpretation of these distortions has been given much attention by some eminent psychologists and researchers. Sigmund Freud (1856-1939) (*see* Appendix), the father of psychoanalysis, believed that the unconscious uses symbols in dreams that represent real emotions and feelings. Alfred Adler (1870-1937) (*see* Appendix), originally a follower of Freud, believed that dreams reflect the individual's lifelong drive for power and success. Carl Gustav Jung (1875-1961) (*see* Appendix) was convinced that the symbolism contained in dreams reflected a wider collective unconsciousness and was common to all, regardless of race or culture.

There can be little doubt that dreams do have symbolic significance, and certain archetypal symbols are now quite generally accepted in the field of psychoanalysis. Applying knowledge of these archetypal symbols should do much to enlighten the individual as to the meaning of his or her dreams. Nevertheless, it is important to remember that dreams are very personal, and it is only in the knowledge of the dreamer's own mood and feelings, and also his or her own circumstances, past and present, that dreams become truly meaningful. The A-Z (*see* page 23) will help you in the process of interpretation if you bear this in mind.

Dream Symbolism

Folklore and dream symbolism

Some of the traditional dream interpretations are ancient indeed. Many were used as mystical tools of prediction. Dream symbolism has its place in the ancient folklore of most cultures and a few are mentioned in this book's A-Z (*see* page 23), such as the folklore of gypsies or travelling people, those of the native Americans, the ancient Egyptians, the Chinese, and the early Christians. Many interpretations in this book are included from the work of a strange second century oneirocritic (dream interpreter) and oneiromantic (dream diviner) called Artemidorus Daldianus (*see* Appendix page 279) who wrote a five-volumed book of dream interpretations and predictions. There is also mention of a nineteenth-century astrologer known as Raphael (*see* Appendix) whose speciality was apparently geomancy—the divination by lines or patterns made, for example by a handful of earth (*see* Interpretation of Dreams by the Ancient Art of Geomancy on page 139). They are virtually unknown now, however, it is interesting to note that although much of the writings of Artemidorus were of the dubious fortune-telling property of dreams, the emphasis, and the emphasis of cultural folklore and the folklore of the gypsy interpreters, was on the analysis of the *symbolism* involved which is also the main factor in modern interpretation and dream analysis.

The language of symbols

Language cannot create thought, but must be created by thought. Thus the first expression of articulate thought must have been through symbols rather than through words, for obviously before attempting speech, man must have perceived objects, and their meaning, use and similarity must have established themselves in his consciousness. Spoken words evolved as expressions of symbols. In this capacity they have remained somewhat incomplete, for they merely express ideas and do not originate them. However, our language is rich in conceptual metaphor. *Life is a journey* is a common everyday conceptual metaphor, eg: 'He came to a point in his life where every day was an uphill struggle.' *Argument is war* is also a commonly expressed metaphor, eg: 'He fought his case valiantly.' *Time* is often expressed as if it is a *resource* eg: 'We're running out of time.'

Conceptual metaphor exemplifies how symbolism is innate in language (for a complete explanation of this theory *see Metaphors We Live By*; George Lakoff and Mark Johnson, University of Chicago Press, 1980). In *The Divided Self* (1960), the Scottish existential psychiatrist R.D. Laing, used this type of conceptual metaphor—in this case life, or life's work, as a quest—to describe Freud's contribution to psychoanalysis:

'Freud was a hero. He descended to the 'Underworld' and met there stark terrors. He carried with him his theory as a Medusa's head which turned these terrors to stone.'

The place of the conceptual metaphor in our language goes some way to explain why subconscious thought expresses itself in the disguised form of symbols.

The interpretation of dream symbols

In *The Interpretation of Dreams* (1900), Freud writes of the subject of symbolism:

'For a few kinds of material a universally applicable dream symbolism has been established on a basis of generally known allusions and equivalents. A good part of this symbolism, moreover, is possessed by the dream in common with the psychoneurosis, and with legends and popular customs.'

In *The World of Dreams* Havelock Ellis (1859-1939) (*see* Appendix) likewise commits himself to symbolism:

'It seems today by no means improbable that amid the absurdities of this popular oneiromancy there are some items of real significance.... Where we are faced with the question of definite and constant symbols, it still remains true that scepticism is often called for. But there can be no manner of doubt that our dreams are full of symbolism.'

Psychoanalysis, therefore, admits that there is some relevance to the traditional symbols of dreams. Jung's fascinating, if somewhat cryptic, work likewise abounds in symbolism. Freud's approach to psychoanalysis and the psychodynamics of personality was by turns thought to be revolutionary and was also thoroughly criticized. His emphasis on sexual drive as the main behaviour-determining agent was thought at the time to be shocking and too restrictive even by some of his colleagues. His work on dream interpretation shows this emphasis on sexual symbolism.

All dream interpretation involves drawing upon personal theories. In the desire to establish hypotheses and to demonstrate theories, the interpreter may draw upon a restricted individual viewpoint, ignoring traditional historical and psychological thought of which they have no experience. In translating the meaning of certain symbols and in fitting them upon certain dreams, interpreters might ignore the history of a symbol throughout the centuries. This history may seem irrelevant to the individual, but it goes some way to explaining the universality of some dream symbols.

Tradition should not be dismissed as the mere perpetuation of superstition. The literature, historical writings, philosophy and traditional folklore of many cultures clearly show that many symbols are typical of many different cultures. Symbolism is purposeful and significant, the outcome of inherited memory, tradition and history as well as the individual's own creativity. Tradition, representing the accumulated reasoning of the race from the inception of thought, is the most universal authority for the interpretation of symbols.

The precise translation of dream symbols is, however, very much dependent on the dreamer's own recognition of what the symbol might mean to him or her personally. If you want to take a more esoteric view of this phenomenon, it is the relation of the symbol to the dreamer's own personal myth (a spiritual view of the human subconscious as encompassing psyche, conscious, unconscious, past life and the past itself) as opposed to the universal myth.

The emotions felt by the dreamer during the dream are also vital to its interpretation, as how the dreamer feels about the dream symbol will apply to what the symbol represents.

Freud argued that in sleep the mind allows suppressed material to come forth in a disguised form—the symbol. The symbol itself is known as the *manifest content* while what the symbol actually represents to the dreamer is the *latent content*. When someone dreams of climbing a high mountain we are aware that this symbolizes a struggle in their life (this corresponds to the conceptual metaphor of life as a journey, and the concept of conquering a mountain links this object as a symbol of a person or an endeavour). The innate symbolism in our language equates the physical exertion of climbing with the mental exertion of an ambition or a problem to be overcome. It is very easy for us to equate the language with the visual image in an interpretation. But only the individual knows what his or her struggle is.

In traditional imagery mountains sometimes signify fear and approaching trouble. To the ancient oneirocritic Artemidorus, this dream would have indicated that the dreamer had, or would have, a great trouble to overcome.

This kind of dream is typical for lots of people (*see* TYPICAL DREAMS page 124). In the interpretation of symbols, which are, after all, merely instinctive records of the human psyche, we must consider not only history, creeds and traditions, but apparent trivialities, all of which combine to explain the soul of the culture from which the symbol emanates.

The origins of symbolism

The scale of symbolism is vast and encompasses all areas of life. The symbol is the primitive expression of speechless man, it is also employed by great minds. Beethoven, Raphael, Michelangelo, Dante and Blake have bequeathed the world symbols that will outlast time. The Wise Men in the East with their frankincense and gold, and the person who wears a poppy on Remembrance Day, are alike symbolists, whatever the expression of the symbol. St John, St Paul, Solomon, Daniel and Ezekiel, the Bible, the Book of the Dead and the Zend Avesta express thought symbolically, while the baseball fan who 'puts it over the plate' does likewise.

Although the civilizing centuries have taught man to think in words, in dreams the mind flies backward to its primitive thought and employs pictures, or symbols. Not only do the Chaldeans, Egyptians and the Biblical oneirocritics utilize the ineradicable human tendency towards symbolism, but modern dream interpreters acknowledge its importance. The perplexing imagery of our dream life continues to fascinate us. Even in modern times dream books are still consulted frequently and with as much interest as ever before.

Traditional folklore and changing society

The symbolism of dreams is merely an effort at expression on the part of the dreaming self. Whether these expressions originate in sexual desire, as maintained by Freudians, or in external stimuli as claimed by physiologists, or from the heights of the human spirit as taught by the mystics, the thought comes from the mind of the individual and is imaged in the language of symbolism. This symbol need bear no immediately obvious interpretation, and it could be that the psyche is represented by a symbol that predates mere speech, but the symbol will have a relevance to the dreamer, and the dreamer and interpreter must work together to find its significance.

The older dream interpreters accepted a simple symbolism founded upon human history and the traditions of the people. Modern interpreters employ reasoning and utilize the unique frame of reference of the individual and the influence of the modern age which brings with it new symbols.

During medieval times and during the renaissance people held a totally different point of view from the ages that preceded them, and both modified symbolic expression. Again racial differences bore their influence. Thus the caverns, mountains and groves were temples and places of worship to Egypt and Greece, while the Hebrews regarded them with suspicion and fear; the Apis, or sacred bull, symbolizing the equinox, at that time in the sign Taurus, was the golden calf, abhorred of the Scriptures, and the serpent, personifying wisdom, was to become accursed of man in Eden.

Gypsy interpreters

Gypsies are the most widely known and the most universally accepted of the traditional mystic dream interpreters. Originally derived from Chaldean, Egyptian and possibly Atlantean sources, their symbolism has been modified, augmented or diminished as the case may be, by time and circumstance. After their descent from their heights of hierophantic teachings, legend and symbol sought the humbler folk. Thus, unconsciously the homely traditions and symbols flourished and scattered to the four winds of civilization, like the seeds of the thistle, the floral prototype of gypsies themselves. Their roots in the subconscious have been deep and permanent, and from these fireside tales have sprung the homely symbols that are most frequently employed in dreams. The universality of the symbols is attributable to the nomadic lifestyle of their preservers, the gypsies. Lacking a written literature, they assimilated local surroundings and drew to themselves the spiritual atmosphere of the varied eras, thus modifying the fundamental significance of the symbols. Early paganism, Hebrewism, Judaism, Christianity, iconoclasm, materialism, each in turn has tinted the mutable science of symbols with the fragments of oral tradition. The scientific colour blindness that has led students to ignore this chameleon quality of symbolism has caused misunderstandings of the symbols themselves.

Christian symbolism—the dove

Symbols can be drawn from many origins. The Christian symbolism of the dove is an emblem of the Holy Ghost. It was the favourite bird of Aphrodite (or Venus) and was thought to be very amorous in nature. It has been pointed out that not only the dove, but the fish and the cross, are all phallic or erotic symbols. This has some truth and a modicum of history as authority, but ignores the changing cultures of intervening centuries and the history of the races that have risen and had their fall since the times of ancient Greece. Unquestionably the dove was originally the symbol of Aphrodite, but it was also the least costly living sacrifice that could be proffered to Jehovah of the Jews, hence for many centuries it was the offering of the poor and the humble—a fitting symbol for Christ, who lived amongst and cared for the humblest of people.

The dream of the dove, while defined by Freud as erotic, is translated by the gypsies as a Holy dream and a good one, and probably in the everyday subconsciousness of the ordinary person, it bears this latter meaning.

The cross

The cross, unquestionably one of the oldest symbols, is of phallic origin. It is now, however, inextricably associated with the Passion and sacrifice of Christ. The image of the sacrifice of Christ and the crucifixion is infinitely more powerful than its original symbolism and has passed into almost every culture in the world. The modern dreamer, Christian or not, who sees a cross in a dream regards it as a symbol of self-sacrifice or of his or her own feelings of religious guilt. Rarely indeed does the dreamer's thought hark back to prehistoric days when the holy emblem bore a phallic significance.

The fish

The adoption of the fish, held by primitive pagans as a symbol of fecundity, was, according to Hulme, adopted by Christians for the reason that the initials of Jesus Christ, the Son of God, are the Greek letters for the word fish. Bishop Kip of California in his work, *The Catacombs of Rome*, corroborates Hulme's theory of the fish as a Christian emblem with the statement that the symbols adopted by the Christians of that day were selected for the purpose of misleading the persecutors of the new faith as well as to convey a message to its followers. They would scarcely suspect beneath the symbol of Aphrodite the meaning that the dove and the fish bore to the followers of Christ.

When dreams 'go by contrary'

The gypsy symbolism lacks the salacious quality usual in that of the Freudian psychologist, and their interpretations manifest a large share of the humour that perhaps the psychologist is lacking. This humour is demonstrated in the interpretation of the dreams that 'go by contrary'. The gypsies also demonstrate a working knowledge of the Bible and a shrewd comprehension of the psychological hypothesis of the subconscious self. The latter is especially surprising in view of the fact that the symbols are old, far older than any possible knowledge of the term subconscious. Dreams of anxiety and loss of property or possessions, for instance, are translated as suggesting thrift on the part of the dreamer, and anxiety indicates the concern that accumulates wealth, while dreams of prodigality and lavishness imply to the shrewd gypsy interpreter a self-complacency and wastefulness that naturally results in poverty.

Since the days of Shakespeare, who undoubtedly was familiar with dreams and their interpretations, a dream of money has implied its loss.

'There is some ill a brewing towards my rest,

For I did dream of Money-bags tonight,' wails Shylock in *The Merchant of Venice*.

Dreams of hunger, care and poverty seem invariably to bear a contrary meaning, whether from motives of consolation to the dreamer or whether through the establishment of symbolism in the days of gypsy supremacy when the witch was sent for to comfort my lady in her bower, we may not decide.

The knowledge of the medieval gypsy

The invariably happy omen of every dream relating to the farmer or to agricultural implements pictures the medieval gypsy looking with longing eyes upon the land that he might not own. Implements of trade, especially the trades of the town, on the other hand imply discomfort and contempt. Female domestic occupations evidently rouse the disdain of the wandering tribes, for to dream of a distaff, spindle, needle, pin or any other symbol of a purely feminine occupation implies gossip and mischief.

Apart from these there is still a certain natural and obvious symbolism that establishes itself even more strongly than symbols of past traditions. These symbols are derived from a knowledge of the powers of nature and of natural history, and in gypsy dream interpretations these take, and hold precedence. The goose appears in dreams, not as the sacred bird of the Greeks and Romans, but as an emblem of stupidity; insects denote hurts and stings and animals generally signify misfortune in accord with the naturalist's knowledge of the proclivities of the beasts themselves. Sometimes this natural symbolism is tinged with humour as in the dream of soap which is held to signify transient worries, while the dream of yeast is another example of practical homely symbolism.

Morality

Rigid morality is the general tone of the gypsy translation, the morality of children's fairy tales and of folklore in which the villain is discovered and punished and the good man rewarded. The virtue of hard work is implied in that all manner of work prognosticates success, even when superficial worldly judgment might argue the contrary. A dream of a workhouse is one that forecasts a legacy.

Falsity of every description is fiercely frowned upon by the old-world morality of the dream books. Wigs, false hair and teeth, rouge, etc, invariably connote evil or evil conditions. Physical indulgence is likewise disapproved, and dreams of eating or of food invariably predict illness; whether from a sternly moral disapprobation of gluttony or whether from the modern theory of a physical dream as implying a physical desire, it is impossible to say. Cynical knowledge of human nature is implied in the interpretation of the dream of servants and inferiors into a prediction of hostility, and the interchangeable dreams of tombs and weddings might bring a smile of agreement from the sceptic. With some dream interpreters dreams of marriage herald death, and dreams of death predict a wedding. The phallic and erotic symbols of modern interpreters are invariably translated as ominous dreams by the gypsy.

Artemidorus Daldianus

The list of dream symbols in the following A–Z includes interpretations from several sources. Of the ancient oneirocritics and oneiromantics, Artemidorus Daldianus is the one most generally cited, with Raphael following in importance.

Artemidorus was the 'great lawgiver of the dream world', says one writer upon the subject, and his *Oneirocritica*, a record from the interpretations of the Greeks, Assyrians and Egyptians, was once the statute book of dreams.

He lived in the second century AD under the Emperor Antoninus Pius, and claimed to have gathered his dream lore from ancient and established sources.

He gives certain rules for dream interpretation that it may be well to remember, not only in dream interpretation, but in forming judgment upon the efforts of others in this direction.

'In giving judgment on dreams we are to take notice that dreams are proportioned according to the condition of the party dreaming. Thus those of persons of eminency, be they good or bad, will be great—that is, if good, they signify great benefit; but if bad great misery. If the party that dreams be of a mean condition, the dreams, with their events, will be mean also; if poor, their dreams will be very inconsiderable. For the rules of dreaming are not general and therefore cannot satisfy all persons at once, but often, according to times and persons, admit of various interpretations...

Moreover, all those things which are done by us and to us, and towards us only, we must think that they appertain to us particularly. And on the contrary, that all such things as are not done by us, nor towards us, nor in us, shall happen to others; and yet, notwithstanding, if they be our friends, and the dreams signify good, the joy shall come to us; and if contrary, then the contrary; but if they be our enemies, we ought to think and judge accordingly.'

It is interesting to note that this ancient fortune-teller places an importance on the individual's interpretation of the symbol. We may not believe the predictive element of dream content as Artemidorus and Raphael did but, through the ages, it is surprising to note the similarities between the ancients and the moderns in the approach to dream interpretation.

A-Z of the Language and Symbols of Dreams

A

abandonment someone who dreams of being abandoned by close family may be experiencing greater personal and sexual freedom than he or she has had before. Dreams of being abandoned may also reflect feelings of being unwanted or unloved, feelings of emotional isolation.

abbey this dream is one of comfort, peace of mind, etc. The symbolism of sanctuary is obvious.

abbot, abbess, hermit, monk, nun, or priest to dream of becoming one denotes calmness in passion. Merely to dream of one indicates pride, or malice of which the dreamer will be the victim. The significance of this dream is evidently due to the regard in which the clergy of past ages held their gypsy brethren.

abduction if the dreamer is the abductor, the dream indicates a desire for power. Individuals who dream of being abducted are probably going through troublesome times, and may have a feeling of being carried away by events.

abortion a dream of abortion dreamt by a man reflects feelings of guilt, not necessarily in connection with parenthood or actual abortion. When dreamt by a woman, abortion dreams can indicate anxiety about starting out on something new.

abroad a dream of foreign travel may represent the dreamer's desire to be free of the constraints of his or her present environment, whether by making new friends or significantly altering his or her lifestyle.

abscess, boil, running sore, etc to dream of having any of these afflictions indicates good fortune and good health, preceded by a temporary sickness (Raphael). These dreams may reflect illnesses in corresponding parts of the body. This interpretation is attributable to the theory that these visitations clear the system of impurities, thereby conferring comfort after sickness. *See also* ULCER.

abyss if the dream involves feelings of fear, then it probably represents some loss of control, death or failure, or it may symbolize the dreamer's failure to face up to certain situations. If no fear is present, then a dream of falling into an abyss can represent the potential of going beyond preconceptions and experience. An abyss indicates impending danger, a dream of warning (Artemidorus) or an erotic dream of warning (Freud). This dream may be interpreted as a symptom of vertigo, due to apoplexy, etc. *See also* PRECIPICE.

acacia flowers a dream of rest and tranquillity, say the gypsy dreamers. This is an erotic dream according to Freud, while flower symbolists proclaim the blossom as signifying 'rest to the heart'. The Egyptians held it as sacred to woman.

accident obviously, such a dream could have a link with a real accident experienced by the dreamer, but if no such experience has taken place, then the dream is probably due to anxiety. A dream of an accident at sea, for example, can signify the end of a long-term relationship and the accompanying feelings of insecurity. If someone dreams of coming to grief in an accident it may be that he or she is in fact punishing him or herself for something. Dreaming of an accident befalling somebody else may be indicative of negative feelings towards that person. To dream of injuring any part of the body may indicate suffering in that part (Raphael). In this case the dream is attributable to physical stimuli.

accolades *see* APPLAUSE.

acid dreaming of acid may indicate that something is weighing heavily on the dreamer's conscience, i.e. 'burning into' his or her mind.

acorns the saying about great oak trees growing from little acorns has some validity in the world of dreams, where the acorn is a symbol of potential for great growth, whether it be mental, physical or spiritual. This is a good dream according to Artemidorus, denoting health, wealth and happiness. If single it denotes a happy marriage. Acorns were regarded in certain parts of Europe as a symbol of wellbeing. They also bore a certain significance as associated with the sacred fire in the worship of Zeus at Dodona.

acting dreams of acting and giving a poor performance suggest a lack of self-confidence about something. Dreams of performing may also point to the part which a person plays in life, the act he or she puts on in front of other people.

actions what one is doing with one's body in a dream may be significant.

dancing a dream involving dancing is generally taken to be symbolic of the interaction of people on an emotional or sexual level, even as the precursor to sexual intercourse. It can also reflect feelings of elation, joy or victory that the dreamer experiences in life.

kneeling may denote a feeling of humility or even worthlessness on the part of the dreamer.

lying down may suggest relaxation, passivity, or a denial of responsibilities.

running may suggest a strong sensation of the life force within, and exuberance. Running away suggests avoidance, either of emotions, fears or responsibilities, depending on the context of the dream. A fortunate dream of advantageous journeys and elevation in rank unless the dreamer falls, in which case misfortune is denoted (gypsy folklore).

turning turning round and round in circles suggests indecision and lack of direction. Turning to face in another direction suggests a decision to make changes in waking life.

admiration, adoration to admire others in a dream will not necessarily represent admiration of any one person in real life; it is more likely to represent finding and submitting to some sort of guiding spirit or influence.

adultery, affairs a dream of adultery may relate to a similar situation in real life, or may merely be a sign of unresolved guilt about something completely unrelated. Occasionally, dreams of committing adultery may be indicative of a simple yearning to do just that, but they may also indicate anxiety. A dream of adultery committed by one's spouse may reflect fears of just such a thing, or may reflect the dreamer's fears of his or her sexual allure.

adventure the wild, wonderful and sometimes terrifying adventures that occur in dreams are often a simple release from the reality of our lives, which is usually rather more mundane. If the adventure is terrifying, this normally reflects a desire to escape from a restrictive situation, while being afraid to do so.

aeroplane *see* JOURNEY.

aggression/hostility to dream of being an aggressor is often a simple expression of anger which the dreamer has been forced to suppress in waking life. It is worth reflecting upon why the dream anger is directed towards a particular person or group of people. A woman who dreams of an aggressive man may have a deep-seated fear of sexual assault, while an aggressive woman in a man's dream may, in reality, be a symbol for the unresolved fear of his mother.

alcohol dreams of being drunk and incapable may point to excesses of some sort in the life of the dreamer, or may express a subconscious fear of losing control.

alley loss of property is augured here, a plausible interpretation from the gypsy standpoint, while the Freudian erotic meaning is less obvious.

alligator *see* ANIMALS.

almond to dream of eating an almond symbolizes future enjoyment and travelling in distant lands. If the almonds are bitter the journey will be unhappy. The almond has always been a sacred symbol throughout the orient and can be traced etymologically to *al monde*, meaning Lord of the World, sole protecting Lord.

almond tree a dream of success (Raphael). A symbol with religious connotations, as the almond has. Freudians contend that dreams of trees bear an erotic meaning.

anchor hope fulfilled is the general dream interpretation, endorsed by Christian symbolism. The Japanese hold it as an emblem of security and safety.

angel an angel appearing in a dream is possibly a symbol for the mother of the dreamer, or at least those aspects of the dreamer's mother which exercised a benevolent or benign influence over his or her life. A purely Christian symbol of protection, divine grace, etc, to the dreamer it prophecies peace and unspeakable happiness.

animals dreams of animals are often a reflection of 'the animal within' the dreamer, i.e. motivations and impulses that are of an instinctive rather than an intellectual nature. Certain animals are thought to have special significance.

Freud and others attach sexual significance to dreams of animals; dream interpreters, however, regard the dream of a number of domestic animals as foretelling happiness, while wild animals symbolize enemies.

alligator/crocodile a cunning, dangerous enemy. Being attacked by an alligator indicates the dreamer's insecurity and fear of an enemy. Freudians would translate this as an erotic dream.

ape or *monkey* a dream of deceit, treacherous friends and associates (Artemidorus). Plato taught that the soul of a bad jester would return as an ape. It may be a modern symbol of uncleanness, lust, cunning, and malice. It was, however, an emblem of wisdom in Egypt and of the god Thoth, patron of the art of writing.

baby animals all of us still have certain needs for nurturing which we never grow out of. We all need to be cared for, to a certain extent. These needs are often represented by baby animals in dreams. Alternatively, baby animals could represent immaturity.

bear a bear may be a symbol of motherhood, or perhaps possessiveness. It can signify a rich, powerful enemy. To overcome a bear in your dream is a favourable sign (Artemidorus). Although the cult of Artemis worshipped the she-bear, in Christian thought the ferocious animals are usually suspect. The bear is a modern symbol of ferocity and surliness. A dream of this kind also has a sexual significance.

boar storms and tempests are predicted by this dream, as is trouble caused by evil-minded people (Artemidorus). A Christian symbol of impurity. A sexual symbol of power and oppression (Freud).

camel this is a dream of burdens patiently borne (Artemidorus). The camel is a modern symbol of patience and submission.

cat cats symbolize the elegant and mysterious aspects of some people. Cats also represent intuitiveness. A dream of a cat may be an unfavourable one of treachery and deceit. To be scratched by a cat symbolizes bad luck, but to kill one is a good omen denoting triumph over enemies (Artemidorus). The image of a cat in a dream expresses an angry, discontented mood. The cat was worshipped as a symbol of the sun god in Egypt. The same word, Mau, stands for both cat and light. The Hebrew horror of the gods of the Egyptians is therefore expressed in their interpretation of the cat as a symbol of deceit and treachery. To dream of a *black cat* or any black animal is unfortunate, for these are associated with evil spirits (Artemidorus). The Chinese attach especial misfortune to the symbol of the black cat. American Indians hold it as a symbol of good luck. The *kitten* symbolizes joy, peace and happiness at home; to be scratched by one, however, predicts an unhappy married life (gypsy folklore).

cattle a dream of a herd of cattle is a dream of prosperity (gypsy folklore); a dream of plenty in proportion to the number seen (Artemidorus). 'Cattle over a thousand hills,' we read as the symbol of success in the Old Testament. The *cow* is a symbol of the earth as mother of all things. The *bull* represents urges of a sexual nature, i.e. animal lust. It can also represent aggressive impulsiveness ('like a bull at a gate'). Violent enemies and slander are forecast by this dream (Artemidorus). A dream of a bull, as with many dreams of animals is an erotic dream (Freud and

Jung). To be attacked by one can be interpreted as an omen or as an erotic dream.

It is the Assyrian symbol of royal authority and of the sun, sacred also to the Egyptians and the Romans. Its modern symbolism is strength, yet throughout the whole of the gypsy dream interpretation it bears an evil meaning, due either to the legend of the golden calf, or to the apparently evil construction of all erotic and phallic symbols.

An *ox* in a dream signifies the yoke of obedience. A pair of fat oxen predicts a year of plenty, lean oxen are an omen of scarcity and famine. Oxen ploughing a field predict gain and plenty (Artemidorus). The symbolism is plainly drawn from Pharaoh's dream of the kine. The ox symbolized patience, strength and sacrifice, in Christian art.

chameleon this dream indicates that the dreamer is being cheated mercilessly (gypsy folklore).

clam to dream of digging for them is a good omen, denoting thrift (gypsy folklore).

crab signifies a ruinous lawsuit (gypsy folklore); a modern expression for an ill-tempered person; the tenacity of the crab has become symbolic.

deer dissensions, disputes and quarrels with one's sweetheart (gypsy folklore). It can also be an erotic dream (Jung). To dream of a *fawn* denotes inconstancy (gypsy folklore). The fawn is a symbol of fleetness and timidity. To kill a *hart* in your dreams forecasts an inheritance from an old man, also the overcoming of fugitive and deceitful enemies. A running hart shows wealth through subtlety (Artemidorus).

dog dogs appear quite frequently in people's dreams. Their symbolism rather depends on the way they appear in the dreams. Thus, friendly dogs can represent faithfulness and friendship, either of the dreamer or another person, whilst vicious dogs can represent aggression and betrayal. The dog is a modern symbol of fidelity. *Bulldogs* represent faithful, loyal friends (gypsy folklore). To dream of following *hounds* denotes unprofitable pursuits (gypsy folklore). A dream of a *mastiff* is one of a strong, powerful, but unknown, friend. To be bitten by one predicts an injury from a friend (gypsy folklore). Jung and Freud classify all dreams of animals or of being bitten by animals as erotic, or sex dreams.

dolphin out of water, a dream of the loss of sweetheart or friend; swimming it augurs unexpected adventure. In medieval art it symbolizes social love. The dolphin was anciently held as the special friend of man and the saviour of the shipwrecked.

donkey/ass/mule the most basic life-force within the dreamer, i.e. the reflexes which are necessary for life may be represented by an ass or a donkey. To dream that mules are savage and mad and that they hurt denotes deceit by someone of your own household (Artemidorus). *Ass* a dream of patience that will enable the dreamer to overcome all obstacles. A Christian symbol of humility and patient endurance.

earthworm a dream of secret enemies (gypsy folklore).

eels a warning to beware of uncertain speculations (gypsy folklore). 'As slippery as an eel,' is the old simile for a rogue.

elephant a fortunate dream forecasting riches (gypsy folklore). The elephant is a symbol of power and wisdom. In India the god of wisdom is elephant-headed.

elk a dream of good luck (gypsy folklore).

ferret a dream of enemies deep and sly (gypsy folklore). The symbol is founded on the reputation of the ferret as being a sly and wicked creature.

fish fish in dreams represent the unconscious motivations or impulses of human beings, either individual or collective, and are often closely connected with the unconscious drive to procreate. Fish may represent unknown aspects of the self that are as yet undiscovered or not yet understood, or may symbolize a supreme being, such as the Christ figure. Dreaming of eating fish can be symbolic of an attempt to find the hidden self by delving deep into the unconscious. Fish can predict much pleasure, and comparative independence (Raphael). Originally an emblem of sex and of fecundity it was adopted by the Christians as a symbol of Christ and the church.

frogs a lucky dream, forecasting good to all conditions (Artemidorus). The frog is a symbol of transformation, regeneration, new life, resurrection. However, if the feeling that accompanies the dream of frogs is revulsion then the dreamer must consider what aspect of their life might be making them unhappy.

goat a dream of enemies, trials and deceit (Artemidorus). The goat is an emblem of lewdness and wickedness in Christian symbolism.

hare a dream of wealth resulting from fertility of resource and address. The hair is a symbol of nimbleness, wit and cleverness in gypsy folklore and African lore.

hedgehog a dream forecasting the meeting with an old friend whom you have not seen for years (gypsy folklore). The hedge-hog is a gypsy emblem of honesty and loyalty.

hog avarice and greed are indicated by a dream of a hog (Artemidorus). The hog is a symbol of sensuality.

horse the appearance of a horse in a dream is generally thought to represent human dynamic energy, whether mental or physical, sexual or creative. A wounded or a dying horse will therefore represent the weakening or fading of power in some way. Dreaming of running away from a horse or horses can mean a fear of the dreamer's own potential in some way, whether this be his or her sexuality or intellectual, spiritual or physical potential. Jung regarded this as an erotic dream. To dream of riding signifies success (gypsy folklore).

hyena a dream of cruel sorrow (gypsy folklore). The hyena is a symbol of ferocity.

jackal this dream denotes an enemy who will backbite and bring trouble (gypsy folklore). An Egyptian symbol of judgement, and of watchfulness over sacred things, the jackal was evidently held in horror by the faiths that succeeded those of Egypt.

kangaroo dreaming of kangaroos signifies prolonged worries. To kill one is a lucky dream (gypsy folklore). Wild animals generally symbolize misfortune with gypsy interpreters. Freud and Jung, however, attach to them an erotic significance.

leeches to dream of leeches being applied denotes sickness (Raphael). As an ancient and popular remedy, the application of leeches would indicate a subconsciousness of illness, though this is unlikely in the modern age.

leopard to dream of a leopard signifies dangers and difficulties and as many changes as there are spots on his coat (gypsy folklore). The leopard is the symbol of watchfulness and alertness, also treachery.

lion lions mean power, particularly the power and strength brought on by anger and aggression. This is also true of a dream of a *wolf*.

Dreaming of a lion is said to denote discourse with a great king or commander. Combat with a lion forecasts a quarrel with some great adversary, and the lioness signifies the same as the lion, only that carried out by women. 'I have known by a dream of a lioness tearing or biting that rich personages have fallen into crimes and accusations.' (Artemidorus). Strength, majesty and courage are symbolized by the lion. In Egypt the overflow of the Nile occurred when the sun was in Leo, the constellation of the lion. Hence the lion's mouth became a symbol of waterspouts, etc.

lizard misfortune through secret enemies is denoted by this dream (Artemidorus). The lizard is the medieval symbol of misfortune and ill-luck.

lobsters foretell sorrows and troubles (gypsy folklore).

lynx a dream warning you that you are watched by a keen-eyed enemy (Artemidorus).

mare for a man to dream of seeing a young mare denotes marriage to a beautiful, young, rich woman. An ill-shapen mare denotes a disadvantageous alliance (Artemidorus).

mouse a dream of mice denotes envious slanderers and poverty (gypsy folklore).

otter a dream of disagreeable and dangerous acquaintances (gypsy folklore).

oysters 'To dream of opening and eating oysters shows great hunger, or a living earned through pains and difficulty.' (Artemidorus).

oyster shells empty oyster shells signify loss, disappointment and worry (gypsy folklore).

panther a dream predicting the approach of evil, a lawsuit (gypsy folklore); the panther is the symbol of watchfulness and alertness.

32

pig a dream both good and bad. Dreaming of a pig may denote false friends, but a faithful lover (gypsy folklore). The pig is a Chinese lucky symbol, but is regarded as an emblem of greed.

porcupine a dream auguring the handling of a delicate affair (gypsy folklore).

racoon to dream of a racoon is a sign of rain (gypsy folklore). The Ainu, the aboriginal people of Japan, prayed to the skulls of these animals during drought to bring on rain. To increase the storm they donned gloves and caps of racoon skin and danced.

rat dreaming of many rats signifies enemies through whom the dreamer will suffer losses, trouble and anxiety. To kill rats, however, is a good dream (Raphael).

reindeer always a lucky dream (gypsy folklore). The association with the Christmas legends accounts for this interpretation.

salamander a dream of assurance that neither man nor elements can harm you (gypsy folklore). The symbolism here is derived from the traditional belief that mythical beasts was that they lived in fire.

salmon a dream denoting division in the family (gypsy folklore).

scorpions misfortunes through secret enemies (gypsy folklore). The scorpion is an ancient symbol of war.

shark this dream denotes an enemy. If the shark eats you, the enemy will ruin you (gypsy folklore).

sheep/lamb to dream of sheep predicts prosperity and enjoyment. If they are scattered they signify persecution (gypsy folklore). The *lamb* was an early Christian symbol for the church. A dream of a ewe-lamb symbolizes a faithful and precious friendship (gypsy folklore). 'A possession greatly prized' in scriptural symbolism. A dream of a lamb is always a favourable dream except to dream of slaying a lamb, this denotes moral torment. To own a lamb denotes comfort, peace and happiness (gypsy folklore).

shellfish to find shells empty, loss of time and credit; to find them full, hope of success. To gather them, merry making and sport (gypsy folklore).

shrimp a dream of grief and distraction.

snail to see a snail in your dream foretells honourable promotion. If it shows its horns it denotes infidelity, adultery, want of chastity, etc. (Artemidorus).

snake could reflect fears of plots against the dreamer or sexual anxiety. *See also* REPTILE and SERPENT.

spiders to dream of a spider foretells money. For a spider to spin its web before your face augurs a fortune (Raphael). The spider is the symbol of shrewdness, perseverance and foresight. To dream of seeing the upper part of a room covered with spiders may be a symptom of headache.

stag a dream denoting gain and profit (gypsy folklore). The stag can be a symbol of solitude (Christian).

tiger this is the dream of an enemy. To escape from the chase of a tiger is a good omen; otherwise the dream predicts ruin (Raphael).

toad a dream denoting a malicious enemy. To kill a toad is said to predict success and triumph (gypsy folklore). The symbol of malice.

tortoise a dream signifying success through long toil and perseverance (gypsy folklore). See Aesop's fable of the hare and the tortoise.

trout a dream denoting money, the larger the trout the more the money (gypsy folklore).

viper enemies who strive to injure you symbolize an unfaithful partner (gypsy folklore). The symbolism here derives from the fable of the man who nourished a viper.

walrus to dream of a walrus denotes a wasted life (gypsy folklore).

weasel a dream of a weasel is said to forecast friendship for malicious persons (gypsy folklore). The symbolism derives from the weasel being an emblem of malice.

whale a dream warning the dreamer of danger (gypsy folklore).

wildcat a warning to beware of enemies who have gained your confidence (gypsy folklore).

worms to dream of seeing worms in the path predicts death to the dreamer or to his friends (gypsy folklore). Worms were a medieval symbol of death and decay.

zebra a dream denoting misplaced friendship and ingratitude (gypsy folklore).

anniversary dreams usually indicate a happy time within the family, a get-together or a reunion.

anus *see* BODY.

ants *see* INSECTS.

anvil an anvil usually indicates prosperity despite obstacles (Raphael). It is an emblem of the primal force.

ape *see* ANIMALS.

appetite dreams involving appetite are generally sexually orientated. Dreams of loss of appetite can mean loss of libido, while hunger or thirst represent great sexual desire.

applause, accolades this is generally a wish-fulfilment dream. The dreamer seeks recognition for something which he or she has achieved. Some would believe that such a dream can foretell good fortune of some kind.

apples *see* FRUIT.

apple tree alive and flourishing, good news; dead, bad tidings. In mystic literature, the apple is the tree of life.

archbishop to see an archbishop in dreams, is a sign of coming death. Gypsy outlaws established this unwholesome symbolism for the mighty prelate.

arms *see* BODY.

arrow this is an ominous dream if the arrow is directed towards the dreamer, or penetrates his body. It indicates that you feel that someone may be plotting against you (Artemidorus). An interpretation obviously derived from the significance of the arrow in warfare. Freudians regard this as a sex dream, probably tracing the symbolism to the arrows of Eros or Cupid.

ashes a dream of trouble and misfortune at hand. Ashes are a Christian symbol of mourning and grief.

ass *see* ANIMALS.

aunt *see* UNCLE.

axe to see an axe in a dream denotes death. Freud designates this as an erotic dream, although the interpretation is rather hazy. Amongst primitive races the axe was the symbol for God or the Divine Being. Later it became a symbol of solar power, with modern times, however, its symbolism altered and it became a crudely murderous weapon.

B

baby babies appear quite frequently in dreams. A crying baby is generally thought to represent illness of some kind. Babies also represent one's responsibilities. Dreaming of looking after a baby and something dreadful happening to it can mean that you are frightened of making a mess of things. Dreaming of giving a baby to someone else to look after will mean shedding one's responsibilities, delegating, or perhaps even letting someone else take the blame.

baby animals *see* ANIMALS.

Bacchus, bacchanalians the interpretation given by Artemidorus of dreaming of Bacchus, the god of wine and drunken revelry, is of a bad year for wine and grape growers.

back to see your own back in your dream indicates misfortune, uneasiness of mind, sickness, etc. This may be a dream incited by backache, and its attendant discomfort that draws the dreamer's attention to that portion of the anatomy.

Artemidorus saw such a dream as a prediction of the love of a child or success in love.

backbite to dream that you are victimized by a scandal promises high success, the favour of great persons. A dream of CONTRARY MEANING, probably inspired by the interpreter's knowledge of the subconscious.

bag *see* SACK.

baggage a dream of weariness, fatigue, an overburdened conscience. This dream might have religious significance being symbolic of the burden of sin.

bagpipes a dream forecasting increase in family and fortune (gypsy folklore). A Carpathian legend was that whenever someone played the bagpipes all things that he desired would grow about him.

balloon in gypsy folklore this dream symbolizes unsuccessful schemes.

balm a dream that denotes sickness but certain recovery (Artemidorus). This may be a dream incited by discomfort in some part of the body.

bamboo a dream of dissension in the family circle in gypsy folklore. Probably originating in the use of rattan or bamboo for purposes of chastisement.

bananas *see* FRUIT.

banner to see the banner of your native country symbolizes misfortune to a loved one or a fatal journey in gypsy folklore. Another representation is that of a military emblem; to see it flying against a clear sky signifies victory over enemies.

barefoot to dream that you have become barefoot is a dream of success and prosperity (gypsy folklore).

barley bread in gypsy folklore, to dream of eating barley bread denotes health, contentment, etc. It is plainly a dream of healthy hunger and its gratification.

barley fields in gypsy folklore, to walk through them indicates trouble and pain to the dreamer. This is distinctly the symbol of gypsies, in view of the penalties attached to damaging the farmer's crops.

bath baths generally represent a kind of moral cleansing, a kind of 'washing away of guilt'. The dreamer may desire to alter his or her habits and adapt a healthier lifestyle.

bathing a dream of bathing in clean, clear water is a dream of great good fortune, in muddy water, the reverse is true (Artemidorus).

battle a battle, or taking part in battles, usually signifies struggles which the dreamer faces in his or her life. To overcome indicates triumph (gypsy folklore). Evidently the realities of warfare were too grim and too close to admit the rule of contraries to apply to this dream, to which modern interpreters, however, attach an erotic meaning.

beacon light a dream indicating deliverance from care and trouble (Artemidorus).

beads this dream denotes success, good fortune, honour and wealth (gypsy folklore). The symbolism is derived from the property of amulet beads to avert misfortune and the evil eye.

beans an unfortunate dream. To eat them augurs illness, to see them growing predicts contentions and quarrels (Artemidorus). An erotic dream according to more recent authority. The symbolism may derive from the Flamen Diates at Rome, the Egyptian priests, the ancient Hebrews and the Pythagoreans who were forbidden to eat them.

bear *see* ANIMALS.

beard to see one in a dream denotes health. If it is a long one it represents gain. A beard on a woman, however, is a disagreeable omen (Artemidorus). The beard symbolizes the male sex and according to Freudians is an erotic symbol representing the genitalia.

beasts *see* ANIMALS.

bed *see* FURNITURE.

bedroom *see* HOUSE.

bee *see* INSECTS.

beetles *see* INSECTS.

behind *see* POSITION.

bells a good dream under most conditions (gypsy folklore). They were believed by the ancients to disperse storms, to drive away pestilence and devils, and to put out fire. In Christian symbolism bells represent the exorcism of evil spirits.

In modern times, however, subject to the context of the dream, the bells can be interpreted as alarm bells, warning the dreamer of something he or she should be paying heed to, or something that he or she is in danger of overlooking.

bicycle journey *see* JOURNEY.

birds birds can signify many things in dreams. Birds in general are thought to represent some aspects of the human being, particularly intellect and spirituality. Some say that a bird in flight represents sexuality, particularly sexual freedom. Freudians regard dreams of birds as erotic dreams. Other interpreters give them varied meanings according to the nature of the birds.

caged birds represent frustration and confinement. *See also* CAGE.

blackbird both in dream lore and in symbolism these birds indicate slander, suspicion and trouble.

chicken for a mother to dream of seeing a brood of chickens under a hen warns her that despite her care some of her offspring will stray (Artemidorus). This dream is traceable to maternal anxiety.

cock a dream denoting pride, success and power, combined with watchfulness (gypsy folklore). The cock is a modern symbol of vigilance, formerly held sacred to the sun. The cock was also the herald of Apollo.

A dream of a cock crowing warns of a false friend, or a betrayal (gypsy folklore). The symbolic connection here is with Christ's betrayal.

crane a dream denoting wickedness on the part of the dreamer (gypsy folklore); the symbolism here is probably derived from the well-known destructiveness of these birds among the fish and smaller varieties of their own species. To the Egyptians it was a symbol of the dawn and of regeneration, while to the Japanese it denotes longevity. Freudians regard it as bearing an erotic significance.

crow a symbol representing death. This is an invariably ill-omened dream. Artemidorus holds it as the dream of an adulterer. Raphael labels it the sign of a funeral. Cicero was warned of his own death by a number of crows circling about his head.

cuckoo a dream predicting disappointment in love (gypsy folklore). The cuckoo, according to Dr Samuel Johnson, is the symbol of faithlessness.

dove the symbol of peace in dreams, just as in life.

The dream of a dove is a fortunate one denoting happiness and fidelity at home (Artemidorus). Originally an erotic symbol as the bird of Aphrodite, it later became the bird of holiness, symbolizing the sacrificial offerings of the Hebrews.

duck a dream of profit and pleasure (gypsy folklore). A symbol of good fortune (Chinese).

eagle power, freedom, perception and domination. An eagle rushing through the air denotes successful undertakings; flying overhead, dignity and honours. To a pregnant woman this dream augurs the birth of a prodigy.

falcon to have one on the wrist denotes honour (gypsy folklore).

goose a sexist interpretation from Raphael is that for a single man this dream predicts a silly and incompetent wife. Modern nursery lore represents the goose as an emblem of silliness, despite that fowl's illustrious reputation in both Rome and Egypt. The cackling of geese denotes good luck and speedy success in business (Artemidorus). The symbolism derives from Roman history, referring to the cackling geese that saved the city.

hawk the dream of the commencement of a new enterprise. If the hawk darts downwards you will succeed, but if a little bird attacks the hawk you will fail (gypsy folklore). The hawk was the ancient symbol of the sun, of intelligence and good luck and also of enterprise. The hawk was the bird of Horus.

humming bird travel in a foreign land and success is symbolized by a dream of this little creature fluttering from flower to flower (Artemidorus).

jackdaw to dream that one crosses your path symbolizes the meeting of bitter enemies. To catch one signifies success in defying enemies (gypsy folklore).

lark a lucky dream forecasting health and prosperity (Raphael). The lark is the symbol of joy and of praise.

magpie a dream of deceit (gypsy folklore). The bird itself symbolizes deceit and misfortune.

ostrich long futile conversations are here denoted (gypsy folklore). The symbolism here is connected with the legend of the stupidity of the ostrich.

owl a dream of an owl denotes unhappiness, sickness and discontent. The hooting of an owl in a dream denotes death (gypsy folklore). The Romans regarded the owl as the bird of wisdom, yet it was an evil portent. In Christian art they symbolize mourning and desolation.

parrot this bird denotes the revelation of secrets, also eavesdropping (gypsy folklore).

partridge to a man this dream indicates dealings with malicious and amoral women (Artemidorus). This bird has ever been held as the symbol of foolishness.

peacock to see one spreading its tail denotes wealth and a handsome wife. For a woman this is a dream forecasting the promotion of her husband to popular favour. To a young woman it symbolizes vanity and the attempted seduction by an unworthy man (gypsy folklore). The early Christians held it as the symbol of immortality. It was also the bird of Juno, who cursed whosoever should pluck its feathers that their children should never be well, nor should men come for their daughters—hence the superstition attached to these feathers. They are the modern symbol of pomp and vanity.

pheasants a dream of inexhaustible happiness. To carry one in the hand denotes health, profit and glory. To eat one in a dream is a reference to surfeit of food and indigestion (Raphael).

pigeon wild pigeons signify dissolute women. Tame pigeons denote honest women and matrons (Artemidorus). For symbolism of pigeon *see dove*.

quail a dream denoting bad news, misfortune (Artemidorus). The word quail was once synonymous for prostitute, owing to the salacious character attributed to the bird.

raven a raven is a symbol of trouble and mischief. In gypsy folklore it is said to be a sign of infidelity. In some cultures the raven is a symbol of knowledge. It was once associated with the god of light, poetry, music, healing and prophecy, Apollo. Modern symbolism regards it as a symbol, of misfortune.

robin a dream of happiness and joy (gypsy folklore). The symbolism derives from the robin being a Christmas bird.

rook a dream auguring business promptly concluded (gypsy folklore).

singing birds foretell joy and delight.

small birds signify lawsuits.

sparrow a good fortune will attend whatever you have in view after this dream (Raphael).

stork a dream of change, possibly loss (gypsy folklore).

swallow news from afar is forecast by this dream. A swallow's nest is a symbol of domestic happiness (gypsy folklore).

swan a white swan denotes wealth and happiness; a black one, grief (Raphael). The swan was a sacred bird of the ancients, although it was a medieval symbol of hypocrisy as the swan has white feathers and black meat. In Norse legend, however, they were held as sacred and still are in Eastern Europe.

turkeys a dream denoting triumph over enemies (gypsy folklore).

turtle dove fidelity, gentleness and good housekeeping in the marriage partner (gypsy folklore).

vulture an evil dream of people trying to destroy your reputation and malevolent rivalry and revenge (gypsy folklore). Here the symbolism is derived from the Scriptures; ancient Hebrews held the vulture in abhorrence, while in Egypt it was the symbol of maternity and of the protection of Isis.

to catch birds with lime denotes unfair triumph over enemies. *See also* FEATHERS.

bird's nest to dream of finding a nest with eggs indicates profit. A nest that is empty, disappointment (Artemidorus); here the symbolism is that of nature itself.

birth dreams of birth taking place can mean some sort of fresh start or major change in the life of the dreamer. For a woman, dreams of giving birth may be wish-fulfilment.

birthday represents happiness or good fortune.

black *see* COLOURS.

blackbirds *see* BIRDS.

black cat *see* ANIMALS.

blood *see* BODY.

blossoming trees an invariable dream of gladness and also of prosperity (Artemidorus). Undoubtedly the symbolism is taken from the gladness of spring, as associated with these blossoms.

blue *see* COLOURS.

boar *see* ANIMALS.

boat journey *see* JOURNEY.

boat, canoe, sailboat, ship, etc seen in a clear stream, this is a dream of happiness. To see one sink indicates disappointment, to fall from one, great dangers, to sail on smooth water, happiness and prosperity; on muddy water, trouble (Raphael). *See also* JOURNEY.

body to dream that your body is robust denotes authority, that it is weak denotes failing or infirmity of the part in question (Artemidorus). The body is generally considered to be representative of the individual. Parts of the body therefore represent aspects of that person.

anus represents the individual's ability to express him or herself and to give of him or herself.

arms represent the potential in the individual for caring and affection. To dream of losing the right arm signifies the death of father, son or brother; of the left arm, of the mother, daughter or sister. To dream that the arms are withered predicts suffering in health and fortune; that they have grown strong indicates success. The latter part of this interpretation is based upon possible physical stimuli, and subsequent effects on the body.

blood can represent menstruation and thus womanhood, or the individual's essential being, the spirit which flows through him or her. To see a quantity of gore or congealed blood is said to predict dreadful calamity or death.

eyes the perceptive abilities of the dreamer. This is a dream predicting success through foresight (Artemidorus). The symbol of the eye is eternal vigilance.

finger to dream of losing a finger shows trouble (gypsy folklore).

hands signify creativity, perhaps sexual creativity.

head the idea which the dreamer has of him or herself, his or her intentions, wishes and beliefs.

heart to dream of the heart as sick or suffering augurs illness dangerous in proportion to the suffering. To dream of an injury to the heart portends danger. Dreaming of heart disease may well be attributable to physical conditions.

knees to fall upon the knees symbolizes a need for help (gypsy folklore).

mouth representative of the dreamer's needs and their fulfilment. It may represent the female genitalia.

nose the intuitive qualities of the dreamer. To dream of a great, fair nose is fortunate and is said to signify subtlety, prominent acquaintances and great personages. Dreaming of a nose longer than ordinary promises wealth and power. Two noses augur discord and quarrels. A stopped-up nose indicates deceit in a domestic circle (Artemidorus). The Egyptian priests believed that a wart on the nose indicated knowledge in proportion to the size of the wart.

penis the essential being of the man; the driving force behind his existence. *See also* GENITALS.

teeth the things with which we bite, and therefore the dreamer's ability to be aggressive. Dreams of teeth falling out indicate a fear of loss of power and of growing old and dying. To dream of loose teeth denotes personal sickness. To lose a tooth denotes the death of a friend or relative. For all the teeth to fall out forecasts your own death (gypsy folklore). *See also* TYPICAL DREAMS.

throat to dream of cutting someone's throat augurs unwitting injury to that person (gypsy folklore). *See also* TYPICAL DREAMS.

vagina womanhood, femininity, procreative abilities.

wrist to dream of hurting the wrist predicts a future injury through a foolish act (gypsy folklore).

boil *see* ABSCESS.

bones human bones are an omen of death in the family (Artemidorus). They are a Christian symbol of death and mortality.

book books in dreams represent wisdom and learning. A book that cannot be opened will signify a secret that cannot be revealed. Open books mean opportunities for learning and changes for the better in one's life. This is a dream predicting the acquisition of both knowledge and wisdom (Artemidorus). The book is a Christian symbol of hidden wisdom and of learning.

boots if new, they symbolize a happy future. Boots or shoes are symbols of luck.

bottle dreaming of a bottle, especially if it is one full of wine, denotes joy, celebration and drinking to someone's health. A broken bottle symbolizes disappointment (Artemidorus).

bow *see* ARROW.

box to dream of opening a box and of looking for something that you cannot find augurs disappointment in money matters (gypsy folklore). The interpretation here is derived from a knowledge of the subconscious desire to search for and to find money, an anxiety dream. It can also signify a coffin and death.

If the dreamer dreams of a plant box or a window box, the dream denotes long life, prosperity and a happy family (Artemidorus). It is a symbol of long life, perpetual hope.

bracelet dreaming of a bracelet is supposed to be a prediction of a wealthy marriage. A dream of an amulet is a dream of happiness and success.

brain this dream symbolizes sickness, loss of reputation, or some kind of weakness (gypsy folklore).

brambles or **briars** a dream of desire in love, a wish for the unattainable (Artemidorus). It is interesting to note that Freud and modern interpreters corroborate this interpretation, that thorned bushes symbolize that which is sexually unattainable.

branches branches with leaves and buds symbolize happiness and joy.

break any dream of breakage implies misfortune.

limb to break a limb denotes sickness.

furniture denotes loss of money.

mirror to break a mirror or looking glass is a symbol of death.

window a broken window is a prediction of danger of fire (gypsy folklore).

The logic of these interpretations is plain, the breaking of a limb is a forewarning of pain, possibly not yet noted by the waking consciousness, fear of financial loss readily expressed in the destruction of property. By the same token the warning of fire, subconsciously read and noted while the consciousness was unaware might readily be construed as a broken window, symbolizing a means of escape. The superstition of a broken mirror as predicting misfortune predates written history.

bride or **bridegroom**, **bridesmaids**, **ushers**, these dreams may have an erotic interpretation. According to Raphael they are dreams denoting grief and disappointment (but he invariably places an unfortunate interpretation upon all dreams of an erotic nature). The appearance of a bride or bridegroom in a dream will tell the dreamer something about his or her thoughts and desires in relation to finding a lifelong partner. Seeing someone else as a bride or bridegroom may mean that you fear losing their friendship to someone else.

bridge dreams of bridges denote changes, how you view the bridge in the dream will explain how you feel about the particular transition taking place.

crossing a bridge to see oneself crossing the bridge denotes work and possible anxiety in store.

broken bridge a broken or rickety bridge is an expression of fear about possible trouble ahead and a warning to take no steps on an unknown road.

falling may be stimulated by physical reasons (*see also* TYPICAL DREAMS). The symbolism of a bridge spanning water is obviously the subconscious hope of success. Falling expresses the anticipation of failure.

brood *see* BIRDS.

brooks clear and near the house, an honourable office in which the dreamer will practice benevolence; muddy brooks indicate loss. Dried up brooks augur ruin to their owners (Artemidorus).

brown *see* COLOURS.

bugle to hear a bugle indicates unexpected good news (Artemidorus).

bull *see* ANIMALS.

bulldog *see* ANIMALS.

buoy this dream is a warning of danger ahead (gypsy folklore).

burglary dreaming of being burgled often means a fear of losing something precious, either something material such as one's home, or something more metaphysical, such as one's independence or self-confidence. *See also* TYPICAL DREAMS.

burial *see* CONTRARY MEANING.

butcher to dream of a butcher cutting up meat denotes trouble and sickness (gypsy folklore). It may be a dream of physical stimuli originating in the organ the butcher seems to be cutting.

butterfly *see* INSECTS.

C

cabbage to dream of cabbages growing denotes health and long life. The eating of them denotes sorrow, loss and illness (gypsy folklore). The former version of the dream, like all dreams of growing things, is optimistic, the latter may be an indication that you are bored and see your life as dull.

cage without birds a dream of a cage denotes trouble. With birds the dream denotes contentment and happiness. A cage with the door open and the bird flown, the dream signifies desertion by the lover or husband. To see a bird escape augurs an elopement (Artemidorus). Cages, and things in cages, generally represent restrictions or frustrations to individuals, perhaps to their ambitions or their sexual desires. *See also* BIRDS; ENCLOSURE.

camel *see* ANIMALS.

candle to see one being lit forecasts a birth. To exhibit a lighted candle predicts contentment and prosperity. To dream of making candles symbolizes joy and satisfaction. To see a candle burning brilliantly denotes prosperity, health to invalids, and marriage to single people. A dimly burning candle shows sickness, sadness and decay (Artemidorus). The symbolism is that of the sacred flame, the vital spark, with the sacredness invariably depending upon the fiery element.

Men who dream of flickering candles may have concerns about their sexual potency.

Brightly burning candles may mean a desire on the part of the dreamer to find fulfilment in a spiritual way.

candlestick this dream forecasts an invitation to a wedding (Artemidorus). Here the ecclesiastical association is apparent. The candlestick is an emblem of Christ and His church, and a near universal symbol of ceremonial faith.

canon *see* CAVE.

cannon *see* WEAPONS.

canoe *see* BOAT.

captive a dream of being held captive may mean that you are unhappy in a relationship or in a place of work and feel restricted. *See also* CHAINS; ENCLOSURE; IMPRISONMENT.

car journey *see* JOURNEY.

cards to play them in a dream denotes quarrels and deception of which the dreamer will be a dupe (gypsy folklore).

carp this symbol denotes good luck through work (gypsy folklore). The carp is a Japanese emblem of endurance.

castle castles represent security. The more heavily fortified the castle, the greater the dreamer's desire is for security. It may mean the protection of things that are important to dreamers or the protection of the dreamers themselves.

A dream of a castle is generally a good one. To enter one indicates pleasant hopes. However, to see one burned denotes misfortune, an accident, sickness or death to the owner (gypsy folklore).

castration a man who dreams of castration undoubtedly fears failure and losing his status as a man. Women who dream of castration are probably embroiled in bitter relationships with men and seek to somehow disempower them.

cat *see* ANIMALS.

caterpillar *see* INSECTS.

cattle *see* ANIMALS.

cave or cavern, canon, grotto, crypt obscurity and misfortune are interpreted from these symbols (gypsy folklore). Caves and grottoes have an ancient and sacred symbolism, while popular tradition peopled them with dragons and other evil creatures. The cave is often seen as the door to the subconscious; the further you go in, the closer you get to your individual subconscious being. Freud saw the dream of the cave as reflecting sexual desires or a wish to return to the womb.

cedar to dream of cedar denotes happiness, joy and peace (Artemidorus). The cedar of Lebanon, by its height, perfume and healing qualities, was a symbol of goodness and of the Virgin.

cellar to dream you are in a cellar shows that you are threatened with illness (gypsy folklore). *See also* HOUSE.

cemeteries cemeteries represent what has gone before; this may in fact be dead people or figures from the past, or it may be a period in the individual's life, or one small incident that is over and done with. Dreams of cemeteries are also prompting the dreamer to think of death and the afterlife and, therefore, spirituality and religious beliefs. The universal acceptance of this as a dream of prosperity suggests either the spirit of contrariety found in certain dream interpretations, or symbolism derived from the morbidity of certain early Christian sects.

48

chaff a dream of abortive or worthless schemes (Artemidorus).

chains a dream warning you against the conspiracy of enemies, from which, however, you will escape (Artemidorus). *See also* CAPTIVE; ENCLOSURE.

chair *see* FURNITURE.

chalice a dream of high ideals and strivings never to be attained in the flesh. This symbolism derives from the chalice as the emblem of the priestly order and of the Grail.

chameleon *see* ANIMALS.

cherries *see* FRUIT.

chickens *see* BIRDS.

chess *see* GAMES.

children to dream of children indicates success (Artemidorus). Children symbolize Christ's love and beneficence. Dreaming that you are a child expresses feelings of immaturity or insecurity.

chimney to dream of one, especially if a fire is lit, denotes domestic joy (Artemidorus).

cholera a dream telling of the likelihood of serious illness (Artemidorus).

Christ to dream of Christ indicates that you are seeking religious consolation or commitment. To dream of Christ on the cross symbolizes trouble and sorrow and may be an expression of religious guilt.

church to dream of building one is an expression of divine love. To dream of entering one symbolizes honourable conduct and benevolence. To talk in one or see it desecrated symbolizes envy, lies and sin. In gypsy folklore to go to church in mourning predicts a wedding; to go in white predicts a funeral (gypsy folklore).

church service a dream of listening to mass, or church music with a feeling of inner peace and satisfaction denotes contentment with one's religious beliefs.

city a busy city predicts riches; a deserted city predicts plague (gypsy folklore). The city is the maternal symbol of woman, who fosters the inhabitants as children (Jung).

clam *see* ANIMALS.

climb a dream predicting successfully overcoming obstacles, and final promotion, honour, etc. (Artemidorus). An interpretation of the character whose subconscious desire is for attainment. *See also* TYPICAL DREAMS.

cloak a dream denoting the concealment of poverty, etc (gypsy folklore).

clock to dream of a clock denotes misfortune (gypsy folklore). The symbolism probably derives from the common superstition attached to the timepiece that it stops at the death of a member of the family, etc.

closeness *see* POSITION.

clothes clothes in dreams may represent the way in which the dreamer appears to the world and to his or herself, his or her self-image and attitudes and the way in which he or she is seen in relationship to other people. Someone who dreams of being wrapped up in a large overcoat, for example, might be protecting, or seeking to protect, him or herself from others, or hiding some aspect of him or herself. Alternatively, such clothing may be representative of the loving protection that the dreamer feels from another, e.g., a mother or a lover.

The *colours* of clothing may also be symbolic in dreams, just as we often dress in different colours according to our mood. Thus, dark dreary colours can be symbolic of unpleasant feelings or occurrences, and black may symbolize death.

Underwear can symbolize the dreamer's feelings about his or her sexuality. *See also* COLOURS.

clouds to dream of heavy clouds signifies threatened misfortune. Light, opaque clouds denote mystery (gypsy folklore). Clouds are sometimes symbolic of the majesty of God, at other times of doubt and obscurity.

clown to dream of a clown predicts misfortune and disgrace (gypsy folklore). The attitude of the medieval world towards the jesters explains this interpretation. To dream that you are a clown reflects the feeling that you are making a fool of yourself in a situation.

club a dream predicting suffering and misfortune (gypsy folklore). Freud regarded it as a phallic symbol. It symbolized strength and power amongst the ancients, bearing no erotic significance. To the Christians it became an emblem of suffering and of martyrdom.

coals to dream of coals denotes trouble, loss and hunger (Raphael). Secret love is the interpretation attached to this dream by Freud. 'With coal no fire so hotly glows as secret love, which no one knows.' (Freud, *Interpretation of Dreams*).

cock *see* BIRDS.

cockchafer *see* BEETLE.

colours it is possible to dream in vivid technicolour, muted colours or monochrome, or one may have a dream in which one colour predominates, most commonly white or black. The colours in a dream can have considerable significance, depending on the state of mind of the dreamer and the context of the dream. *See also* CLOTHES.

black is the colour of the dark, hidden, gloomy and secret. It may be symbolic of death or of a fear of death. The dreamer may be feeling sad or depressed.

blue is a spiritual colour, it may symbolize hope and faithfulness, or reasoning and higher intellect. A predominance of dark and/or dull blues, however, can signify depression.

brown is associated with excrement, dreariness and depression, but also with money, or even gold.

green is associated with growth, both physical and spiritual, and also with things that grow.

red is associated with anger, danger and warning. It may also be a symbol of sexual arousal in certain contexts.

white is associated with purity, cleanliness and innocence. It also has connections with illumination of the mind. White liquid, in certain contexts, may symbolize semen.

column an unfortunate dream (gypsy folklore). Freud regards this dream as bearing a phallic significance. Christians regard the column as an emblem of the Passion.

comet a dream of death and illness (Artemidorus). The omen is apparent in legend connected with these heavenly bodies.

conflict any sort of conflict that is dreamt about has to be considered in the light of what is going on in the life of the dreamer. Victory in conflict, while dreaming, may be wish-fulfilment and some sort of compensation for the individual's inability to overcome a struggle in daily life.

contrary meaning some dreams, according to the ancient oneirocritics and the gypsy interpreters, have a contrary meaning to the expected interpretation. This is the case for some dreams of VIOLENCE, DEATH, burial and financial gain or loss. For example, violence may signify deep affection, and dreaming of a burial may in fact denote a WEDDING. The dream of a wedding may also signify a FUNERAL. A dream of great RICHES may signify imminent POVERTY and vice versa.

corkscrew a dream signifying an inquisitive friend.

corn a dream of riches (Artemidorus). Ears of corn are a symbol of the Holy Eucharist (Clement). An ear of corn is also the symbol of Horus bringing light and plenty to the world.

cornucopia a dream of abundance (gypsy folklore), the Horn of Plenty of ancient tradition.

corridor dreams about buildings or parts of buildings, such as corridors, are often very symbolic. The corridor may be interpreted as the birth canal, a passage from one stage of life to another, or a means of escape from a situation. Bunyan had a dream of a long narrow corridor leading to the sunny side of a far mountain through which he had great difficulty in passing. This signified a difficult religious journey and is said by the poet Southey to have inspired the former's work *The Pilgrim's Progress*.

cow *see* ANIMALS.

crab *see* ANIMALS.

crane *see* BIRDS.

cravat or tie this might predict a sore throat. To take off or remove a tie or cravat indicates the cure of a cold (gypsy folklore). This dream refers to a troublesome partner from whom the dreamer longs to be freed (Freud). *See also* CLOTHES.

crescent a dream interpreted as signifying successful love. The symbol of Isis and of motherhood. In Egypt it is used as an emblem of the Virgin Mary.

cricket *see* INSECTS.

crocodile *see* ANIMALS.

cross to dream of a cross predicts success and honour; to carry it, trouble (Artemidorus). The dreamer may be seeking the comfort of religious consolation.

crossroads dreaming of crossroads may have associations with taking major decisions in life and of choosing from between two or more options as to which course of action to take.

crow *see* BIRDS.

crowd of people importunity, excitement (gypsy folklore). 'This dream is a sign of great excitement in the unconscious, especially in persons outwardly calm.' (Jung).

crown A dream of reward among all people. 'To bear a gold crown on the head signifies the friendship of your liege, honour, pleasure and many gifts' (Artemidorus). The unvarying symbol of reward.

crutches an adverse dream predicting illness (Artemidorus).

cryst *see* CAVE.

cuckoo *see* BIRDS.

cucumber a dream symbolizing serious indisposition (gypsy folklore). Freud believed that dreams about food had a clear sexual significance and the cucumber may be a rather too obvious phallic symbol. If a man has this dream he may fear sexual inadequacy; for a woman it could express a wish for a masculine kind of power.

cupboards *see* FURNITURE; HOUSE.

cupid a dream of love and happiness (Artemidorus)

cypress a dream of sorrow and mourning (Artemidorus).

D

daffodils a gypsy dream of good health and good news.

dagger foretells death and suffering, unless you dream of grasping it firmly, which symbolizes success. Jung interprets the dagger as a phallic symbol.

daisy a good dream in spring or summer, predicting a true lover, but a bad one in winter or autumn (Raphael). The daisy symbolizes the eye of day and the sun.

dancing see ACTIONS.

dandelion this dream denotes secret enemies at work against you (gypsy folklore). The interpretation probably derived from the fact that farmers regard the flower as a nuisance.

danger dreaming of being in some sort of danger or of having a strong sense of danger is one of the ways in which particular anxieties may be manifested in dreams. This may be a fear of letting oneself go emotionally or sexually and so risking betrayal or loss, or it may be fear of coping with some hurdle that is being, or is about to be, encountered in life. Such dreams need to be considered closely in the light of what is going on in the dreamer's life and his or her personal fears, whether acknowledged or hitherto subconscious.

darkness the darkness represents the unknown and also what is depressing or even feared. However, where darkness is dreamt of in association with feelings of warmth and comfort, it may be symbolic of the time before birth and the safety of the womb. A dream of warning against treachery, false friends, and a wilful blindness to reason and good sense (Artemidorus).

dates *see* FRUIT.

day a dream of a clear day is a good omen (Artemidorus).

daylight, daytime *see* TIME.

dead people when one dreams of a person who is already dead, one is likely to be trying to resolve feelings about that person that are as yet unresolved. *See also* TYPICAL DREAMS.

death dreaming of the death of someone may indicate feelings of anger towards that person, even a desire to sever relations with him or her and thus be free of them. It is not likely to mean, however, that the dreamer wishes the person dead.

Dreaming of one's own death may be an attempt to deal with one's own uncertainties and fears about death or it may signify a wish to free oneself of certain current responsibilities or problems. *See also* CONTRARY MEANINGS; TYPICAL DREAMS.

deer *see* ANIMALS.

déjà vu this means literally 'seen before', and is a phenomenon whereby the individual will recognize something that they encounter in life as having been seen in a dream before. In many cases the person or place will have been seen before but has simply not been remembered. Nevertheless, there are cases in which people will, for example, know what is about to happen or recognize where they are going on a journey because they remember similar events or places from their dream life. There is no simple explanation as to why this happens, but it is believed by some that feelings of *déjà vu* are connected with reincarnation and are not so much rooted in dreams as in a previous life of the individual concerned.

delicacies see VIANDS.

deluge overwhelming business loss (Artemidorus). Financial affairs are usually indicated by storms, rain, etc. *See also* RAIN.

departure dreaming of leaving somewhere or somebody has significance in relation to changes in the dreamer's life, a 'leaving behind' of old attitudes maybe, or a major change in lifestyle.

descent dreams of going down from a high place towards the ground may be symbolic of a descent 'back down to earth' in terms of one's approach to life or some particular problem. Dreaming of descending into the depths of a tunnel or cave can either mean an attempt by the individual to reach deeper within the mind and increase self-awareness, or it may represent a returning to the experience of life within the womb.

desert loss of friends and wealth are shown by this dream (Artemidorus). Loneliness and isolation are symbolized.

devil the worst possible dream (gypsy folklore). Dreaming of the devil is a subconscious expression of guilt.

dice a dream of enmity, quarrels and business vicissitudes (gypsy folklore).

digging to dig in clean ground denotes thrift and good luck; in dirty or wet ground, trouble; to dig for gold and find large lumps, good fortune; to fail to find it, disappointment (Raphael). Most dreams of honest toil are of favourable augury. *See also* MUD.

distaff a favourable dream (gypsy folklore). The distaff used to be a symbol of women's work.

distance *see* POSITION.

dog *see* ANIMALS.

dolphin *see* ANIMALS.

donkey *see* ANIMALS.

doors doors in dreams can represent opportunities or paths available to the dreamer in life. Thus, a closed door may represent an option that is no longer available to the dreamer, while an open door beckons the dreamer to take a chance or to move forward into a new 'room' in life.

dove *see* BIRDS.

dragon A dream of sudden changes in the worldly condition, riches and treasure (Raphael). In Christian art the dragon symbolizes Satan, or sin. The Chinese regard a dragon, or winged serpent, as the symbol of the Infinite Intelligence, keeping ward over the Tree of Knowledge. A dragon was also the standard of the Welsh, of the West Saxons, of the Phoenicians and of the Chinese Manchu dynasty. The Celts use the word dragon to signify a chief, a dictator in time of danger, and probably the dream interpretation is derived from this symbol.

dreaming of a dream it may happen, particularly in unpleasant dreams, that dreamers 'interrupt themselves' to give themselves reassurance—'it's only a dream'—or to tell themselves, 'this has happened in a dream before'. It may be that what is being dreamt about is particularly hard for the dreamer to cope with, so the unconscious mind is helping the dreamer to keep the dream safely within the confines of the dream world so that it does not have to be faced up to in 'real life'.

To dream of relating a dream indicates that something unusual is about to happen (Raphael). Evidently a struggle on the part of the subconscious to bring the matter before the consciousness.

dregs a dream of poverty, failure and loss (gypsy folklore).

drown an unfortunate dream predicting illness (gypsy folklore). A dream evidently due to some physical cause affecting the breathing apparatus. *See also* WATER.

drugs or drugstore this may be a dream predicting illness (gypsy folklore). Another reason may be that this is a dream inspired by the subconscious knowledge of need.

drum a dream of strife and war (gypsy folklore).

duck *see* BIRDS.

dust a dream of temporary calamity (gypsy folklore). Dust is the Christian symbol of humility and woe, but its effects are obviously temporary and easily thrown aside.

E

eagle *see* BIRDS.

earth as the earth is the source for growth, so earth in dreams signifies where we are coming from, our family roots, and social background. A universally portentous dream (gypsy folklore). The earth as the symbol of the universal mother is curiously at variance with this interpretation of the oneirocritics. It is only to be accounted for by the hypothesis that in their anxiety to escape all implication of idolatry and paganism, the gypsies reversed the symbols of the ancient creeds.

earthquake losses, broken ties, bereavements (gypsy folklore); nature's own symbolism.

earthworm *see* ANIMALS.

eating eating is seen as the satisfying of a hunger, of a sexual or emotional nature. The sharing of food in dreams may be symbolic of the giving and receiving of love, the sharing of affection and/or bodies.

echo false news and absurdity are hereby indicated (Artemidorus). Dreaming of an echo is likely to be a signal that you are lacking in confidence in some respect.

eclipse Dreaming of an eclipse of the sun predicts a great loss. An eclipse of the moon is not a bad dream as such but whatever your wish is you will not attain it (Artemidorus). The symbolism here is apparent.

eels *see* ANIMALS.

eggs eggs are symbolic of the potential of the individual, which has yet been untapped. A dream meaning happiness; broken eggs, however, predict quarrels and lawsuits; fresh eggs, good news (Artemidorus). An ancient symbol of creation the egg has been held as an emblem of good fortune by all races.

eight *see* NUMBERS.

ejaculation ejaculation is the ultimate end of the sexual act, the final release. Dreams of ejaculation are undeniably sexual and probably represent wish-fulfilment. Ejaculation or, for the female, orgasm while asleep will indicate that the individual has been having a dream that is tied to his or her sexuality, though this may not be immediately apparent through the remembered content of the dream.

elderberries *see* FRUIT.

elephant *see* ANIMALS.

elk *see* ANIMALS.

emerald the dream indicates wealth, a rise in the world (gypsy folklore). Persians used it as a charm against the devil, it also bestows knowledge of the future.

emotion remembering the emotions that were felt while dreaming is essential in unravelling the meaning behind the content of any dream.

enclosure dreams of being enclosed may have connections with the barriers that the individual puts up against the world, the protective 'shell' that is used as a barricade against fears or hurt.

If unpleasant feelings are felt, the dreamer could be facing restrictions to his or her actions and feelings in life and feeling frustrated because of this. *See also* CAGE; CAPTIVE; CHAINS; IMPRISONMENT.

entrails a bad dream predicting sickness (gypsy folklore).

epaulet a dream of dignity (gypsy folklore).

equator good weather and fine crops are promised to the farmer by this dream; to others, abundance (gypsy folklore). The tropical heat here symbolizes fruitfulness.

ermine this dream symbolizes a rise to honour and dignity (gypsy folklore). The ermine symbolizes royalty.

escape dreams of escape may represent a desire to find release from particular circumstances in one's life, or may mean a recovery from depression or even illness.

Dreaming of something escaping from you could be a reminder of something that has been overlooked, or a missed opportunity.

evening dreams of evening may be symbolic of the 'setting of the sun' in one's life, i.e. approaching old age. Alternatively, they can represent times of peace and rest, the calm after the storm and the final relaxation after a period of struggle. *See also* TIME.

ewe-lamb *see* ANIMALS.

exams while exam dreams commonly start in adolescence (a period marked by real anxiety about school exams for most people) they can be repeated over and over again throughout the rest of the dreamer's life, almost always occurring at times of particular stress. The dreams have similar scenarios for most people—turning up at an exam to find that it is not the exam that you have prepared for, looking at the exam paper and finding that it is written in some incomprehensible script or foreign language, discovering that you have to sit an exam for which you have attended no classes, etc. Such dreams are always a pointer to real-life stress and an indication to the dreamer that this stress is a problem that must be dealt with. *See also* TYPICAL DREAMS.

excrement excrement is thought by some to be symbolic of wealth. The link between excrement and wealth has its origins in the belief of early alchemists that all the necessary ingredients for making gold were to be found in faecal matter.

Dreaming of incontinence may indicate a fear of letting oneself go in some way, perhaps a fear of one's emotions.

Excrement in dreams can also signify feelings of disgust towards the self or another, depending upon the context of the dream in which it appears. *See also* MUD.

execution a person who dreams of his or her own execution may be depressed and suffering from severely diminished self-esteem. This could be a way of seeking self-punishment.

explosion dreams of explosion can represent outbursts of anger from which the dreamer feels prevented or inhibited in real life. Such dreams may be symbolic of orgasm, EJACULATION and the culmination of sexual desire.

eyes *see* BODY.

F

failure like EXAM dreams, dreams of failure are generally linked to fears and problems in the dreamer's life. The dreamer may be coming to realize that what he or she is striving for in real life is, in fact, impossible. However, the dream may simply be an expression of fears that the dreamer feels unable to admit to. *See also* EXAMS.

fair this dream predicts coming into the company of many people through whom you will profit (gypsy folklore). Here the gypsy interprets according to his own custom and tradition.

fairy a dream of riches and independence to the poor, to the rich it shows temptation (gypsy folklore). The providence of nursery legend and mythology, their dream symbolism is apparent.

falcon *see* BIRDS.

falling dreams of falling are quite common. Often the dreamer dreams of falling and then wakes up before hitting the ground. Falling can represent any one of several things. Where the dreamer falls and lands, the dream may be sexually related, the fall representing the act of intercourse. Alternatively, a fall in a dream may represent a 'fall from grace' in the dreamer's life; the dreamer has let him or herself down in some way. Approaching some sort of edge and falling over may indicate that the dreamer is heading for problems in life, while dreaming of being in danger from falling can mean that the dreamer has real fears of potential disaster. *See also* TYPICAL DREAMS.

falling leaves *see* TREE.

family for most people the attitudes and values that they grow up with are related to and even dependent on their family. Whether an individual grows up to accept or to reject the values and attitudes of his or her family, it is generally true to say that they have built up their own set of values based on what they have seen and learnt within the context of family life. Equally, the way in which an individual behaves in relation to other people will, in all probability, be rooted in the patterns of behaviour of his or her parents and siblings.

Family figures in dreams may well represent themselves, but they can also represent that part of the dreamer that has its foundations in that particular family member. Thus, a man may have a dream about his mother in which he is perhaps resolving some of his feelings towards her; this dream involves a straight representation of his mother. Or he may have a dream in which his mother represents, perhaps, the caring and nurturing aspect of himself.

Generalizations as to what the appearance of a family member in a dream might mean can have little meaning without first some knowledge of the context of the dream, the dreamer's background, and the influences that have come to bear on his or her life through the family.

Even the fact that an individual may lack a family background (in the traditional sense) is of relevance.

fan a dream of pride (gypsy folklore). A Japanese emblem of authority, power, royalty.

farewell to dream of bidding friends farewell denotes a change in business (gypsy folklore).

farm to dream of taking a farm denotes advancement; to visit a farm and partake of its products, good health (gypsy folklore). Obviously an interpretation derived from the rural districts.

fat to dream of growing fat signals affliction, physical or otherwise (gypsy folklore). It may be the result of physical stimuli, probably the plethora attendant upon certain ailments.

fawn *see* ANIMALS.

fear fear is like all the other emotions that we experience while dreaming in that it can give a real clue as to the dreamer's state of mind, or the dreamer's true response to a situation, or an occurrence in his or her life. Dreaming gives people an opportunity to express feelings that they might otherwise be unable to express properly. Thus, while a person may present a brave, cheerful or perhaps angry face to the world, in dreams he or she can express the fear that lies behind the outward persona. The content of a nightmare, therefore, is not necessarily as enlightening as the fear that has been felt by the person who has had the nightmare. *See also* MONSTER; PANIC.

feathers white feathers foretell success; dark feathers, the reverse (Artemidorus). Feathers are a symbol of power, and in Egypt the emblem of truth, goodness and knowledge. *See also* BIRDS.

ferret *see* ANIMALS.

fever an evil dream of ambitious desires, extravagance, etc (gypsy folklore). The restlessness and delirium accompanying fever would justify this interpretation of a dream undoubtedly attributable to a physical condition.

fields a dream of fertile fields denotes prosperity; barren fields, disappointment (gypsy folklore).

fighting dreams of fighting are indicative of internal emotional, sexual or moral conflict on the part of the dreamer. It may reflect the dreamer's struggle for independence or freedom from a particular situation.

figs *see* FRUIT.

finger *see* BODY.

fire fire can symbolize great passions; anger, a consuming desire for something, or, quite simply, lust. In certain contexts, fire can symbolize enlightenment. A dream of fire can be one of health and happiness. To be burned, however, signifies calamity (gypsy folklore). Sacred to primitive man it symbolizes fructifying strength and heat, the life-giving element. *See also* FLAMES.

firebrand or torch to dream of a firebrand is good for young people to whom it signifies love and pleasure; to see another hold a firebrand is an ill dream for one who would be secret (Artemidorus).

fish *see* ANIMALS.

five *see* NUMBERS.

flames to dream of flames denotes happiness (gypsy folklore). Flames are a Christian symbol of zeal, fervour. *See also* FIRE.

fleas *see* INSECTS.

fleet to dream of a fleet of vessels promises fulfilment of hopes (gypsy folklore). Ships symbolize hopes both in ancient and modern symbolism.

flies *see* INSECTS.

floating dreaming of floating suggests a certain loss of control, involuntary or otherwise, and the idea of letting oneself be carried along by life rather than living it in a more active fashion. *See also* TYPICAL DREAMS.

floods *see* DELUGE.

flowers flowers in dreams will often have strong sexual meanings. In general, they are symbolic of life and growth; also of beauty, love and tenderness. More specifically, a blossoming flower may represent the female genitalia, a bud the penis or vagina. Damaged flowers may symbolize damaged innocence, loss of purity/virginity, while wilting flowers may indicate the decline of sexual/reproductive powers. Joy is indicated by dreaming of flowers in season, but usually the dream augurs disappointment, white flowers are but slightly unfortunate; yellow flowers forecast painful difficulties; red flowers indicate death (gypsy folklore). Freud regards this as a purely erotic dream. In Christian symbolism flowers symbolize immortality; cut flowers, however, are emblematic of death. *See also* TREE.

flying to dream of flying is to dream of release from the influences that are holding one back. These may be practical difficulties, such as lack of money, stifling of creativity in one's job, or family commitments. It could also indicate repressive emotions or a lack of belief in oneself. For some, dreaming of flying may indicate a desire for sexual release. Flying signifies freedom and independence and also the ability to take a different view of the world and of other people. Invariably a happy dream, auguring beautiful things to come. Modern dream interpreters, however, classify it as a typical dream induced by vertigo, etc. *See also* TYPICAL DREAMS.

fog dreaming of fog indicates a problem of perception for the dreamer and a need to look at something more closely in order to understand it fully. A dream of uncertainty (gypsy folklore).

food food represents nourishment, whether for the body, the

mind or the spirit. Dreaming of eating food is symbolic, therefore, of satisfying some desire for nourishment of some sort.
Thus, to dream of sharing a meal with someone may represent
the sharing of mutual love and respect or it may represent the
act of sexual nourishing, i.e. sexual intercourse.

foreign countries dreams of foreign lands may be indicative
of new experiences in life.

forest a dream of dire trouble and sorrow (Artemidorus). The
legends that people the forests with witches, ogres and giants
account for this interpretation. To dream that you are hiding in
a forest suggests that you are guilty about something or have a
secret. Being lost in the forest expresses feelings that you are
going in the wrong direction in life. If the forest is covered in
brown, dead leaves this may express the feeling that a situation
or a relationship is unsatisfactory.

forge a dream of brilliant success through hard work (gypsy
folklore).

fountain to dream of a clear fountain indicates abundance to
well persons and health to invalids (Artemidorus). The fountain
is a symbol of the gospel and of miraculous healing waters. *See
also* WATER.

four *see* NUMBERS.

fratricide success will never attend the dreamer of this dream
(Raphael). The interpretation of what is evidently regarded as a
wish dream.

frogs *see* ANIMALS.

frost to a man in business, a dream of frost predicts difficulties in
trade. To others it may symbolize love nipped in the bud, etc.
See also ICE.

fruit fruit, like flowers, are symbolically linked with life, growth
and sex. Fruits, in particular, are associated with reproduction
and coming to maturity or ripeness. A dream of unripe fruit
may represent sexual immaturity. *See also* ORCHARD; TREE.

 apples ripe apples symbolize success in trade, love, etc. Green apples symbolize the contrary. The gypsy influence is distinctly traceable in the folklore of the apple as a symbol. It confers immortal
youth in the fairytale, golden apples, love apples, etc, while in

Christian symbolism it represents the fall from Eden, the sin that made Christ's coming necessary. It may denote a cunning and dangerous enemy. The apple has long been regarded as a symbol of sexual love and Freudians translate this as an erotic dream.

bananas to dream of eating them denotes misfortune (gypsy folklore). A Melanesian legend, that the banana was the cause of human mortality, may be the source of the symbolism.

cherries to dream of cherries growing denotes health and fertility. To gather them indicates deception by a woman; to eat them denotes love (Artemidorus).

dates a dream of dates denotes either strong and powerful enemies or admirers of the opposite sex (Artemidorus).

elderberries a dream of good luck, speedy marriage and success financially (Raphael). The fruit of the sacred elder, these berries were highly esteemed by the ancient Prussians as symbols of good fortune.

figs a dream of joy and pleasure. Dreaming of figs out of season denotes grief. To eat figs predicts loss of fortune or shame and dry figs signify the slipping away of wealth, but success in married life (gypsy folklore). In sacred symbolism they denote prosperity. They were held as sacred by the Romans, a symbol of fruitfulness and life, and also an erotic symbol.

gooseberries many offspring and the accomplishment of plans are denoted by this dream (Raphael). The gooseberry is an ancient symbol of reproduction and fertility.

grapes eating grapes denotes cheerfulness and profit. Treading grapes indicates the overthrow of enemies; gathering white grapes, gain; gathering black grapes, damage (Artemidorus). They are the symbol of joy, happiness and fertility.

greengages to dream of eating these plums denotes trouble and grief (Raphael).

melon to a sick person this is a dream of recovery by reason of the juiciness which dispels fever (gypsy folklore). This is a dream originating in physical stimuli indicative of coolness and moisture after fever.

olives to dream of gathering them denotes peace, delight, happiness to all conditions. Eating olives predicts a rise in circumstance (gypsy folklore). They are the emblem of peace and plenty.

oranges a dream of tears and anxiety (gypsy folklore); the symbolism is obscure.

peaches to dream of them in season denotes contentment, wealth and pleasure (Artemidorus). They are a Chinese symbol of longevity and good fortune. The peach-tree was also the symbol of the Paradise of Osiris.

pears a dream denoting sickness (Raphael). It was held as an emblem of the human heart.

pineapple someone who dreams of pineapples will soon receive an invitation to a celebration or a wedding. This dream also denotes prosperity and good health (gypsy folklore).

plums green plums forecast sickness; ripe ones are fortunate. To dream of picking plums from the ground and finding that they are rotten indicates false friends, poverty and disgrace. (Raphael).

pomegranate to dream of gathering them ripe denotes fortune through an influential person. Unripe pomegranates foretell sickness and scandal (gypsy folklore). The pomegranate was the Christian symbol of the resurrection and of fertility. With the golden bells they form part of the symbolic robe of the Israelite high priest.

prunes a dream denoting health and joy (gypsy folklore).

raspberries to dream of eating them denotes remorse and sorrow (Raphael). Raspberries look a bit like miniature hearts and for this reason were christened the berries of Eraspe, or Father Eros.

strawberries indicate good luck or a happy marriage (gypsy folklore).

vines to walk under or to pick their fruit is a dream of abundance, wealth and fecundity (gypsy folklore). The spiritual symbol of fruitfulness.

watermelon a dream of sickness (gypsy folklore).

funeral the funeral of a relative or a great lord is a good dream; betokening either a wealthy marriage or a fortune through relatives (Artemidorus). A wish dream (Freud). *See also* CONTRARY MEANING; TYPICAL DREAMS.

furniture/furnishings furniture in dreams may represent, in general, our emotional baggage, or the feelings and attitudes with which our lives have become furnished through our up-bringing and our interaction with others.

More specifically, certain items of furniture are thought to be significant in their own way. A *bed*, for example, may represent one's life as one has made it and one's level of happiness within that life. It may symbolize relations with other people, sexual or otherwise according to the context, marriage, occupation, etc. In some cases, where the mood of the dream is depressing, a bed or lying in bed may signify illness or a need for peace and retreat from the pressures of the outside world. Dreaming of *lying in bed* and watching things going on all around can indicate a certain passivity in one's approach to life. *See also* MATTRESS.

Cupboards or *wardrobes* often hold sexual significance; the cup-board can be the womb. Finding something in a cupboard may signify discovering some aspect of one's sexual self. Alterna-tively, the cupboard may simply represent the mind, the depths of the cupboard standing for the deepest recesses of the psyche. Locked cupboards indicate secrets, or hidden thoughts; an as-pect of the self that is hidden from the world or that is unac-knowledged by the individual.

Dreaming of sitting in a *chair* may reflect a rather passive role in life for the dreamer, or a relaxed attitude.

future dreaming of events that are about to happen is a phe-nomenon that is much written about but, as yet, is little under-stood. It is believed by some to be a manifestation of the sub-conscious link between human beings, whereby strong feelings towards a person may give us an insight into the direction his or her life is taking them. However, this does not fully explain such dreams, as some dreams like this are not about people who are linked to the dreamer in any obvious way. Cynics would explain the phenomenon as being no more than coincidence.

G

gadflies *see* INSECTS.

gallows paradoxically the gypsies saw this dream as fortunate, the dreamer will rise proportionately to the height of the gallows (gypsy folklore).

gambling *see* GAMES.

games games in dreams can reflect the individual's attitude to life and the strategies that he or she develops to cope with certain situations.

Competitive games can symbolize a sense of struggle within the dreamer, a feeling of having to overcome competition from others to achieve goals in life.

Games like *chess* are indicative of a more intellectual approach, a consideration of strategies to employ in working towards one's ends.

Dreaming of *gambling* may be indicative of a certain recklessness in the general behaviour of the dreamer and can serve as a warning to change one's ways.

garden gardens in dreams represent the 'inner person', the feelings and ideas that 'grow' within the individual. Thus, an untidy garden can be seen as a mind that lacks order and perhaps suffers from indecision or lack of purpose; alternatively, it may represent a person who does not listen or pay attention to his or her inner self (i.e. a neglected garden equals a neglected self). A very tidy, symmetrically arranged garden might be seen as a sign of a highly ordered mind, very controlled, perhaps inhibited, while a beautiful garden can reflect a happy state of mind and contentment. Some would say a beautiful garden shows great happiness in the future, while an overgrown or untidy garden points to aspects of the individual's life needing attention.

gardener a dream of good luck and speedy success (gypsy folklore); agriculturists generally connote good fortune in gypsy symbolism.

garlands a dream of triumph (gypsy folklore).

gate a gate, or gates, may be interpreted as the entrance to the dreamer's inner self, the way in to the unconscious motivations of the individual. To go through the gate is to take the opportunity to increase one's self-awareness.

A gate may also be seen as the way into the dreamer's conscious desires, the way to achieve his or her ultimate aims. The interpretation of the dream will very much, depend on whether the gate lies open or closed, what, if anything, is seen to lie beyond the gate, and how the dreamer feels about his or her life at the time of dreaming.

geese *see* BIRDS.

gems a dream forecasting a rise in social position (gypsy folklore). *See also* JEWELS.

genitals genitals in dreams are often symbols of the dreamer's sexual self; a woman, for example, may dream that she has a penis, and this could be interpreted as her experiencing the male part of herself. *See also* BODY.

ghosts ghosts in dreams may either represent the dreamer's individual self, memories of the past that may be tormenting the dreamer, or things that he or she may feel guilty about.

Dreaming of the ghost of a person who is well known to the dreamer may point to the fact that the dreamer is still influenced, whether consciously or subconsciously, by the attitudes and opinions that the dead person had.

giants giants frequently appear in the dreams of children; they most likely represent grownups (who do seem huge to young children). Adults who dream of giants are possibly harking back to their childhood. Alternatively, and particularly if the dream is frightening, the giant may be like a MONSTER and so represent something of which the dreamer has a deep-seated fear and which looms large in his or her thoughts. *See also* MONSTER; OGRE.

gifts the giving and receiving of gifts in dreams should not be seen in a material sense but as the giving and receiving of love or the sharing of thoughts and ideas, or even actions that have certain effects on people. What is given, of course, need not always be pleasant; a nasty gift could be interpreted as something hurtful that is done by the 'giver' in the dream to the 'receiver'. *See also* PRESENTS.

goat *see* ANIMALS.

God one need not be a religious person to dream of God, or even of meeting God in some shape or form. Someone who dreams of God may indeed be in the process of analysing his or her own religious beliefs in life, particularly in relation to life and death; nevertheless, the God in the dream may simply be representative of some figure of authority in the dreamer's life. This may reassure the dreamer that responsibility does not lie with him or her alone, i.e. the buck does not stop with him or her. Alternatively, it may act as a reminder to the dreamer that the power to change things, or the ultimate control, does not actually lie in his or her hands.

Lastly, the appearance of God in a dream can take the place, to a certain extent, of the dreamer's conscience, bringing to the dreamer's attention the moral responsibility that he or she must bear for his or her actions. *See also* RELIGION.

gold gold in dreams rarely foretells untold wealth. It is more likely to represent things of a metaphysical nature that one values in life. Thus, false or tarnished gold will stand for values that are not worth having. To dream of gold embroidered garments indicates joy and honour, to wear a gold crown signifies royal favour; to gather up gold and silver signifies deceit and loss. To dream of pockets full of gold betokens but little money (Artemidorus). Gold was the emblem of the sun and of the goodness of God.

gondola *see* BOAT.

goose *see* BIRDS.

gooseberries *see* FRUIT.

gore *see* BODY.

grain a dream of prosperity. To see large grain bins in a storehouse is a symbol of plenty. A field of grain denotes profit; to harvest grain predicts wealth; to carry it signifies weariness (Artemidorus).

grapes *see* FRUIT.

grass to dream of walking through fields of grass signifies happiness and fortune. To dream of grasses such as sorrel lettuce, etc, denotes grief and embarrassment. To eat grass symbolizes sorrow and sickness. Dead or withered grass denotes misfortune (gypsy folklore).

grasshopper *see* INSECTS.

grave dreams of graves may be indicative of the dreamer's coming to terms with his or her own mortality, or the grave in the dream may represent some aspect of the dreamer's life, or character, that has changed or been overcome.

green *see* COLOURS.

greengages *see* FRUIT.

grindstone success through toil is indicated by this dream (gypsy folklore).

grotto *see* CAVE.

ground to fall to the ground predicts humiliation and disgrace (gypsy folklore).

grove this dream denotes trouble but to a lesser degree than the dream of a FOREST (gypsy folklore).

guilt like many emotions experienced while dreaming, the guilt that a dreamer is feeling may well be guilt that is being repressed, or should be felt, for the dreamer's thoughts, words or deeds in real life.

guitar to dream of listening to a guitar signifies happiness (gypsy folklore).

gun to dream of a gun is an expression of anxiety about a sexual experience. To hear the report of a gun denotes the death of a friend, a slander, enmity and loss (gypsy folklore). A dream of a pistol is one which predicts attacks from secret enemies (gypsy folklore). *See also* WEAPONS.

gypsies dreaming of gypsies may indicate an unexpressed desire for more freedom in life. This may be physical freedom or freedom of the intellect or the spirit.

H

hail to dream of hail denotes sorrow and trouble, with tempest and thunder it denotes afflictions. It predicts tranquillity to the poor, however, for during storms they rest (Artemidorus).

hair dreams of hair refer to the dreamer's feelings about their freedom and their standing in life.

long hair someone who dreams of having long, flowing locks may have a yearning for more freedom than he or she currently has. If a man dreams that he has long hair like a woman this reflects feelings of effeminacy and weakness. If the hair is longer and darker than usual, this predicts an increase of riches.

black and short hair this dream is said to predict misfortune.

dishevelled hair this denotes annoyances and sorrows.

hair falling out denotes subconscious feelings of insecurity. A bald-headed woman symbolizes famine; a bald-headed man, abundance, riches and health (gypsy folklore). If the hair is thinner than usual then this predicts affliction and poverty.

hair in a tangle this dream symbolizes quarrels in which the dreamer is the losing party, possibly the outcome of a lawsuit.

white hair to dream that you have white hair denotes high honour. Seeing it grow white may predict loss of fortune.

hammer a dream of oppression (Artemidorus). 'Like a hammer that breaketh the rock in pieces,' *Jeremiah xxiii*.

handbills to post them denotes dishonour. To read them denotes labour without reward.

hands *see* BODY.

hanging to dream of being hanged predicts success in proportion to the size of the gibbet. If the dreamer is ill he will find joy and contentment. The dream of condemning another to be hanged signifies anger with someone. The Persians and Egyptians interpreted the dream of hanging as predicting riches, honour and respect. To dream of being delivered from being hanged forecasts downfall in estate and dignity (Artemidorus).

hare *see* ANIMALS.

harpies tribulation and pain caused by envious persons, malice and treachery (Artemidorus).

hart *see* ANIMALS.

harvest a dream of prosperity (gypsy folklore).

harvesters many harvesters denote success in trade; to see them idle is a symbol of scarcity (gypsy folklore).

hatchet a warning to expect peril or death (gypsy folklore).

hawk *see* BIRDS.

hawthorn a dream of constancy (gypsy folklore).

hay or hay-cart this dream denotes success through diligence (gypsy folklore), and is an agricultural symbol of prosperity.

head *see* BODY.

headache a dream of trouble, illness, and poverty (gypsy folklore). The physical stimuli account for this interpretation.

health a bad omen for the sick (gypsy folklore), evidently due to physical stimuli.

heart *see* BODY.

heat heat is generally thought to symbolize the heat of strong feelings, either sexual arousal, romantic love or perhaps anger. It should be considered within the context of the dream. The dream may also have a physical cause.

heather or **heath** a dream of hope; if withered or dry, frustrated hopes (gypsy folklore).

heaven a beautiful and auspicious dream. To ascend thereto symbolizes grandeur and glory (Artemidorus). This need not be a religious dream. It could signify that you aspire to something better in life; this may be for spiritual reasons or something as mundane as wanting a new job.

hedgehog *see* ANIMALS.

hedges when green, this signifies prosperity; when thorny and impenetrable, dangers and difficulties (gypsy folklore). Freud would have given this symbol a sexual significance, signifying the dreamer's fear of sex, or feelings that it is forbidden.

height dreams of being at a great height, on top of a mountain or a particularly high building maybe, point to feelings of isolation on the part of the dreamer. It may indicate achievement or success, but this could be success that makes the dreamer stand out from his or her peers. *See also* MOUNTAIN and POSITION.

A dream of looking up at something that is high above may indicate a feeling of smallness in the general scheme of things.

hell a dream denoting mental agony or bodily pain (gypsy folklore).

hen *see* BIRDS.

herbs to dream of hemlock, henbane and other poisonous herbs denotes that you are in danger, but to dream of useful herbs is a good omen (gypsy folklore). This might be a dream caused by physical stimuli induced by the odours of herbs or other strong smelling scents.

herdsman a dream of damage to the rich and profit to the poor (Raphael). Here the interpretation is based on reason, for what would be gain to one is loss to the other.

herd of cattle *see* ANIMALS.

hermaphrodite dreaming of having the physical characteristics of both sexes is likely to be either an indication of a need to explore one's own sexuality or an expression, within the safety and privacy of one's dreams, of aspects of one's sexuality that one may well be prohibited from expressing, or too inhibited to express, in real life.

hermit *see* ABBOT.

heron or **crane** *see* BIRDS.

hickory-nuts trouble from creditors.

hiding a dreamer who hides may indeed be a dreamer who has something to hide, or who thinks he or she has something to hide. The dreamer may wish to hide his or her true feelings from someone, or may possess a characteristic of which he or she is ashamed. If the predominant emotion felt while dreaming of hiding is fear, then this may indicate that the dreamer is frightened of letting his or her true emotions be felt or shown.

hills climbing a hill in a dream is indicative of a struggle of some sort in real life, either to achieve something or simply to maintain the status quo. Going downhill at speed in a dream suggests a loss of control, or at least a feeling that one is losing control in real life. Gently rolling, fertile, green hills may have a sexual meaning, suggesting in particular the female body, the breasts and belly of a woman of child-bearing years. To dream of climbing a steep hill and reaching the top, difficulties overcome; to fail to reach the top, disappointment; distant green hills, hope, promise (Artemidorus). *See also* TYPICAL DREAMS.

hog *see* ANIMALS.

holly this is a good omen in a dream (gypsy folklore). Holly is a traditional symbol of joy.

holes holes in dreams very possibly have sexual significance, symbolizing in all probability the vagina and womb. Emerging from a hole may therefore be indicative of the process of being born, while entering a hole may be either an expression of desire to return to the safety of the womb or a symbol for the act of penetration in sexual intercourse.

Other interpretations of holes in dreams include death, the unknown and the subconscious.

To determine the significance of a hole in a dream, it must be considered along with the other elements of the dream and the dreamer's current life and mood.

home dreams of home may indicate security and contentment, or may have a more sinister meaning; it all depends on the experiences that the dreamer has had of home.

homosexuality one does not have to be homosexual in order to dream that one is homosexual or taking part in a homosexual act. Dreams give us the opportunity to explore aspects of our personalities and our sexuality that we feel, for one reason or another, prevented from exploring in real life. Dreams of homosexual love may be wish-fulfilment but are not necessarily so. We all need the love of people of both sexes, and yet we may feel inhibited from acknowledging that what we need from people of our own sex is love, even if this is not sexual love but the love of friendship, brotherhood, sisterhood or the love between parents and children.

honey a dream of prosperity (Artemidorus). 'A land flowing with milk and honey,' was the promised land of the Hebrews. *See also* BEES.

hops a dream of peace and plenty (gypsy folklore). The soothing influence of hops is well known and the symbolism may well be derived from this.

hornet *see* INSECTS and STING.

hornet a dream of vexations (gypsy folklore). *See also* INSECTS and STING.

horns a dream of wearing horns denotes dominion and grandeur (Artemidorus). Horns have ever been worn by priests and rulers of barbarous tribes as symbols of state and power. Jung and Freud attach to them a phallic significance.

horror feelings of horror are, like any emotion that can be felt in a dream, genuine feelings. They should be validated, not in relation to the content of the dream, but in relation to that aspect of, or occurrence in, the life of the dreamer to which the dream symbol is alluding.

horse *see* ANIMALS.

horse chestnut a dream denoting home quarrels and worries.

horseshoe a peculiar dream denoting fortune in business and home affairs (gypsy folklore). A world symbol of good fortune.

hospital an unfortunate dream (Raphael). This dream may be a warning from your subconscious that you are working too hard or are getting run down.

hostility *see* AGGRESSION.

hounds *see* ANIMALS.

house the house in a dream is thought to be symbolic of the self, its separate rooms all representing aspects of the self. Thus, the *cellar* and cupboards are the 'hidden self', the deeper recesses of the mind, or the aspects of oneself that one keeps hidden from others. The *bedroom* can either be the parts of one's mind to which one retreats when stressed, or it can be the aspects of the self that one shares with few others; the intimate, sexual self. The *kitchen* is the source of all nourishment, the way in which one seeks and finds fulfilment of all needs, physical and mental. The *walls* of the house are one's mental protection against life. *See also* WALL. To build a house predicts profit, and to be in a strange house denotes change (gypsy folklore).

howls to hear howls in a dream is an omen of death (gypsy folklore). Popular superstition concerning howls is responsible for this interpretation.

humming bird *see* BIRDS.

hungry dreams of feeling hungry may point to some unfulfilled need in the dreamer's life.

hyacinth a dream denoting riches (gypsy folklore).

hydra to see a hydra or seven-headed serpent signifies temptation (Artemidorus). *See also* SERPENT and MONSTER.

hyena *see* ANIMALS.

hyssop a dream signifying labour, trouble, sickness and weakness. To physicians, however, the dream is a favourable one (Artemidorus).

I

ice ice is symbolic of physical or emotional coldness. It may point to lack of love or loss of libido. The dreamer should consider his or her life to try to understand where this coldness originates. It may be a result of the sleeper's body becoming too cold. *See also* FROST.

icicles to a young woman this is a prediction of marriage to an old and wealthy man (gypsy folklore).

idiot to dream of turning into an idiot and going mad predicts favour with princes and also gain and pleasure through things of the world (Artemidorus).

illness dreams of illness may be the dreamer's first 'admission' that all is not well. The problem is not so frequently a physical one as one within the mind. It is possible that the illness represents unpleasant feelings of some sort (guilt, loneliness, etc) that may have been festering for some time, or even depression. Alternatively, to dream of being ill (and hence of needing to be cared for) can denote a need for attention, affection or real caring in the dreamer. A dream of someone else being ill is possibly an exploration of the dreamer's feelings towards that person; the outcome of the 'illness', the dreamer's emotions and the part that he or she plays in the scenario will all, therefore, be of significance.

illumination some great joy at hand is predicted by this dream (gypsy folklore).

imprisonment the person who dreams of being imprisoned is very possibly suffering from some form of restriction to his or her independence in real life; problems such as restrictive family relationships (particularly those between parents and their children), claustrophobic love affairs, or guilty feelings may be holding the dreamer back from achieving freedom of action, movement or even thought. *See also* ENCLOSURE and CAPTIVE.

imps a dream denoting disappointment (gypsy folklore). The imp is a symbol of malice.

incense a dream of flatterers, parasites, etc (gypsy folklore).

indigence a dream of becoming indigent indicates sudden gain (gypsy folklore). This is probably based upon the caution of the provident and therefore successful person.

infection as in the case of illness dreams, dreams of infections such as ABSCESSES, boils or festering wounds may reflect something within the mind of the dreamer that is bothering him or her, thus 'infecting' his or her thoughts. This may be no more than an irritation that has to be dealt with, but it can also be something of a more serious nature; for example, guilty feelings or negative feelings towards another person for one reason or another.

infernal things to dream of an infernal spirit is a bad sign, indicating death to the sick, melancholy to the healthy, also anger, tumults, illness (Artemidorus). This dream is conceded by physiologists to result from outward stimuli. It may be a subconscious expression of guilt.

infirm to dream of seeing a person becoming infirm, indicates you, yourself, will become so (gypsy folklore). A dream inspired by physical weakness.

insects depending on how the insects are perceived in the dream, the interpretation of their appearance can differ. Buzzing flies may represent nothing more than a nagging problem within the dreamer's mind. The appearance of insects accompanied by feelings of displeasure or disgust will therefore reflect something about which the dreamer is more troubled. The problem may be a sexual one, in that the dreamer may associate both insects and sex with feelings of distaste. In some dreams, insects or small creatures may be representative of one's children; thus, the mother who dreams of insects flying away from her may be dealing with her feelings about her children gaining independence and leaving the family home. A dream that may signify illness and loss (Artemidorus).

ants to the tradesman this dream augurs success. In medieval symbolism ants typify industry. Plato says the souls of unimaginative persons return to earth as ants.

bee a dream signifying both good and bad: good if the bees do not sting, bad if they sting. Seeing bees indicates profit to country people and trouble to the rich.

beekeeping to dream of keeping bees augurs profit.

flying a bee flying about the ears signifies harassment by enemies.

honey and wax such a dream symbolizes sickness or a recovery from sickness. If you dream of bees making honey in the house this predicts dignity, eloquence and success to the occupants.

industrious bees their hard work is auspicious to ploughmen and to those profiting from this industry, to others this dream signifies trouble by reason of the noise they make.

stinging bees to be stung by a bee denotes vexation and trouble. Wounds or injuries are indicated by the position of their STING.

Some bee symbolism may derive from classical mythology. Jupiter is said to have been nourished by bees, and in his infancy Pindar was supposedly fed on honey instead of milk. They were sacred to Artemis and they appear on her statues and on her coins. Mahomet admits bees to Paradise. In modern Christian art bees symbolize industry. *See also* STING.

beetles this dream signifies that you believe some slander is circulating concerning you. To kill the beetle is to overcome this slander (Raphael). The symbolism surrounding the beetle is ancient indeed. It was held as sacred by the Egyptians as a symbol of virility, new life and of eternity. The beetle has been known to be a Christian symbol of blindness.

butterfly lack of fixed purpose, restlessness, inconstancy (gypsy folklore). It was the Greek symbol for the psyche or soul, and the Christians also employed it as a symbol of the resurrection. The significance of its bursting from its chrysalis into glory, was, however, lost during the middle ages, when a more shallow symbolism became established and continues to the present day. Its modern symbolism is that of playfulness, fickleness and living in pleasure.

caterpillar trouble through secret enemies is predicted by this dream (gypsy folklore). Although ancient symbolists classified it with the butterfly as an emblem of the soul, modern interpreters regard it as the secret enemy, symbolized in the way it destroys leaves and vegetation.

cricket (the insect) a pleasant meeting of old friends is symbolized by this dream. Superstition holds this insect as a pleasant omen. Pliny mentions it as much esteemed among the ancient magicians.

fleas a dream of annoyance and discomfort (gypsy folklore). Probably the result of physical stimuli.

flies dreaming of flies predicts troublesome persons who will scandalize you (gypsy folklore).

gadflies a dream of trouble in store for the dreamer (gypsy folklore).

grasshopper a dream prognosticating poverty due to lack of energy on the part of the dreamer (Raphael). The symbol of improvidence.

hornet a dream of vexations (gypsy folklore). *See also* STING.

locusts a dream forecasting extravagance, misfortune and short-lived happiness (gypsy folklore).

maggots as is the case with dreams of INFECTIONS, ILLNESSES, insects etc, dreams of maggots point to some intuitive feeling that the dreamer has that something is not right; either something is causing mental disquiet, or some physical problem is requiring attention.

mosquitoes persecution from petty enemies (gypsy folklore).

moths a dream of moths denotes a love affair in which the dreamer will suffer betrayal (gypsy folklore). The proverbial moth and flame is symbolized in this dream.

wasps to dream of being stung by wasps, a dream denoting envious enemies (Artemidorus). *See also* STING.

invisible an invisible presence, i.e. someone or something that cannot be seen but that is nevertheless active within the dream, is possibly symbolic of some influential authority figure.

iron to dream of being hurt with iron signifies damage. To dream of trading in iron with strangers predicts losses and misfortune (Artemidorus).

island an island may be a symbol of loneliness or a feeling of isolation on the part of the dreamer, or it may be interpreted as a desire to cut oneself off from others. A third possible interpretation of the appearance of an island in a dream is that the island represents the unborn child, and the water surrounding the island stands for the amniotic fluid in which the foetus floats. In gypsy folklore it is a dream predicting isolation and loneliness.

ivory this dream predicts abundance and success (gypsy folklore).

ivy a dream of strong trust and friendship (gypsy folklore). Ivy is a symbol of the Trinity and of the triple creative power, also of loyalty and friendship.

J

jackal *see* ANIMALS.

jackdaw *see* BIRDS.

jailer dreams of IMPRISONMENT are symbolic of restrictions to the freedom of the individual. Therefore, a person appearing in the role of a jailer in a dream will stand for the source of that restriction. This is by no means necessarily another person; it may be the attitudes or inhibitions of the dreamer himself or herself. *See also* ENCLOSURE and CAPTIVE.

jasmine a dream of true love and success (gypsy folklore); a poetic symbol.

jaundice a dream of sickness and poverty (gypsy folklore).

jewels jewels or *treasure* appearing in a dream are unlikely to represent material fortune of any kind. They are more likely to stand for that which the dreamer holds to be valuable in life in a non-material sense, for example, moral values, freedom of thought and creativity, family or romantic love.

To find treasure is a dream of success (gypsy folklore). One of the few dreams involving material gain that is not a dream of CONTRARY MEANING, the reason probably lies in the fact that treasure and its discovery so frequently figures as the traditional reward of virtue in fairy stories and in mythology. *See also* GEM.

journey most obviously, dream journeys can represent the 'journey of life', or a particular stage in life, such as childhood or marriage. Thus a journey that is particularly hard will reflect a difficult period in life. To dream of passing through difficult territory and emerging into easy terrain can reflect a change for the better in life and the overcoming of past obstacles. Those who dream of losing their way and feel frightened and bewildered on their journey are perhaps lacking direction in their lives, or may feel that events are taking such a turn as to leave them without control.

aeroplane journeys may stand for a swift transition between one part of the dreamer's life and another.

bicycle can refer to a difficult phase of life that has to be overcome.

boat the extent of difficulty experienced in a dream of travelling by water can reflect the extent to which boundaries have arisen in the dreamers life. Sailing over smooth water predicts prosperity; rough water indicates misfortune. If the boat is a small one this is said to predict sudden wealth (Raphael).

car can be a symbol of desire or sexuality. There should be particular importance placed on whether the dreamer is driving or being driven, since this is a reflection on the dreamer's sense of independence.

train the way in which the dreamer is travelling may indicate the individual's energy, sexual or otherwise. For men the dream generally has a sexual content especially (using that old Freudian cliché) if the train enters a tunnel, for women it may express a desire for more power. *See also* RAILWAY.

uphill to travel uphill denotes advancement with difficulty.

wood travelling through a wood is a dream of trouble and hindrances.

judge and jury these are often symbolic of the way in which we judge ourselves and our own actions; alternatively, they can represent the influences that have shaped our personal morality. To dream of coming before a judge indicates malice, persecution, etc (gypsy folklore). This interpretation probably stems from the gypsy's experience of injustice and prejudice regarding their way of life.

jump a jump from one place to another may be interpreted as a chance that has been taken or that would be worthwhile taking in life. A failed jump represents either a fear of not succeeding in something or the realization that one has made an error in life.

juniper to dream of felling a juniper tree indicates good luck; eating juniper berries warns against unwise associations.

justice a good dream (gypsy folklore).

K

kangaroo *see* ANIMALS.

kettle a bright kettle denotes success in everyday life (Raphael). Its symbolism would derive from denoting the gypsy way of life.

key a key can indicate the solution to a problem, that which opens up the door to success. Alternatively, it may be that which has been keeping repressed emotions locked up within the dreamer. A third possible meaning for a key in a dream is sexual, the key possibly standing for the penis, and the keyhole representing the vagina. Also a dream of coldness and hindrances to travellers. Fortunate for managers of other people's affairs; to dream of giving a key augurs marriage; to receive one, honour and confidence; many keys denote wealth; to lose keys denotes anger and misfortune (gypsy folklore). A talisman of power, sagacity and foresight. The key is a Chinese symbol of prudence.

kidnap a generally ill-omened dream. A dream of one's own kidnap is a warning to the dreamer to beware. To dream of perpetrating a kidnap is also a warning against others.

killing to dream of killing someone is unlikely to mean that you wish anybody any real harm. It is more likely that the person who is being killed in the dream is a symbol for some aspect of the dreamer's self that he wishes to repress, change or eradicate. Thus, dreams of killing may indicate a feeling of self-loathing.

To dream of being killed may point to some factor in the dreamer's life that is in some way stifling the dreamer or making him or her feel helpless. *See also* MURDER and TYPICAL DREAMS.

kiss a kiss in a dream may be seen in general as an acknowledgement or acceptance of something. Thus, a dream of kissing somebody goodbye can be read as the acknowledgement of the need for some sort of transition in the waking life of the dreamer.

To kiss a relative in a dream denotes treason; a stranger, a speedy journey; the earth, humiliation; the hand of a person, friendship, good fortune; the face of a stranger, rashness followed by success (gypsy folklore).

kitchen *see* HOUSE.

kite a dream predicting elevation in life; should the string break this predicts sudden downfall (Raphael). This dream may well express a wish to escape or to better oneself.

kitten *see* ANIMALS.

knave to dream of being a knave signifies wealth; to be connected with them, lawsuits (Artemidorus).

knee *see* BODY.

kneeling *see* ACTIONS.

knife a knife in a dream is very possibly a sign of aggression on the part of the dreamer, a desire to inflict pain, although not necessarily physical pain, on somebody. A knife that is used against someone but with no effect may reflect feelings of powerlessness or inadequacy in the dreamer.

In certain contexts, a knife may represent the male libido or aggressive sexual feelings. An unfortunate dream, bright sharp knives connote enemies.

knife-grinder to see one foretells robbery (gypsy folklore). This occupation was a common one amongst the gypsies themselves.

knight in armour a dream of peril to come (gypsy folklore).

knitting a dream denoting wicked talk or gossip (gypsy folklore). The domestic occupations of women frequently bear this meaning.

knots knots can be read as problems with which the dreamer is struggling in waking life. There may be a confusion of emotions concerning some aspect of the dreamer's life. A dream of embarrassment and perplexity (gypsy folklore); 'a knotty problem,' etc. The knot is a Chinese symbol of longevity and luck.

L

labourer a dream denoting happiness, increase of fortune, etc (gypsy folklore). The labourer is symbolic of frugality and prudence.

laces to wear them in a dream forecasts disappointment in some new garments (gypsy folklore).

ladder the ladder may represent a path in life that the dreamer is about to take. Climbing a ladder in a dream suggests that the dreamer is aware that there are hazards that have to be faced if goals in life are to be attained. Occasionally, a ladder may have sexual significance as a metaphor for an erection.

This is also said to be a dream of advancement; to ascend denotes elevation; to descend predicts a downfall (Artemidorus).

lake *see* BROOK.

lambs *see* ANIMALS.

lamp to carry a bright one denotes success and this is an especially favourable dream for lovers. A dim lamp denotes sickness;

a light that goes out or is extinguished denotes death; or at least danger (Raphael). In ancient symbolism the lamp or flame represented the vital spark of life. Truth, righteousness and illumination are symbolized by the lamp in scriptural art.

lance a dream of trouble and tragedy (Raphael). The lance is a phallic symbol and therefore this is an erotic dream (Jung). The lance was a Christian symbol of martyrdom and a Greek symbol of the god Mars.

lantern to dream of carrying one on a dark night foretells riches. To stumble while carrying the lantern denotes trouble. If the light is darkened or extinguished then poverty is predicted (Artemidorus). Lanterns can symbolize leadership and it is the Christian symbol of piety and truth. The tarot gives it as a symbol of wisdom.

lark *see* BIRDS.

laurel a dream betokening victory and pleasure (Raphael); symbol of victory.

law, lawyers a dream forecasting heavy business losses. After having this dream be careful about entering into bargains or contracts (Raphael).

leaves TREES covered with fresh leaves signify success in business. Blossoms and FRUITS among leaves are a dream of marriage. Withered leaves signify losses and bad crops (Raphael).

leeches *see* ANIMALS.

leers *see* ONIONS.

leopard *see* ANIMALS.

leper a dream of shame and infamy, it also predicts illness (gypsy folklore).

letter letters may be symbols of intuitive feelings; an unopened letter would therefore represent that the dreamer is 'not listening to his heart'. Opening letters represents the achievement of greater self-awareness.

In certain contexts, an unopened letter may be interpreted as either virginity (protected) or sexual immaturity, or sexual awareness that has yet to be aroused. To write or receive them, good news (gypsy folklore).

lettuce *see* GRASS.

liar to dream of being called one denotes wealth by questionable means (gypsy folklore).

library to dream of being in a library shows success through wisdom and learning (gypsy folklore).

lifeboat a dream predicting success at the last moment (Raphael).

light to dream of being aboard ship and of seeing a light far off assures one of his or her desires. To dream of holding a burning light in the hands is a good sign, especially to the young, signifying accomplishment of designs, honours and good will to all persons. A light in the hands of another foretells the discovery of mischief and the punishment of the offender.

lightning a portentous dream of war and trouble (gypsy folklore).

lighthouse a dream warning of a danger ahead and the possibility of a mistake in judgement (Raphael). Freudians see this symbol as having a strong sexual significance.

lilies a symbol of innocence, chastity and purity. To dream of lilies promises happiness through virtue (Raphael).

   lily of the valley a dream of humility.

   water lilies signify regeneration and purification.

   lotus a symbol of new birth and of immortality.

   tiger lilies, a dream of the temptation of wealth (gypsy folklore).

limping a dream of limping predicts misfortune and shame (Artemidorus).

linen to dream of being dressed in clean linen denotes glad tidings; soiled linen, poverty, imprisonment, disappointment, etc (Artemidorus).

lion *see* ANIMALS.

lizard *see* ANIMALS.

load a dream of care and toil, to succeed in carrying it signifies the triumph over difficulties (gypsy folklore).

loaves to dream of seeing loaves foretells want (gypsy folklore). Evidently a desire or need is assumed as the latent content of this dream.

lobster *see* ANIMALS.

lock a dream foretelling difficulty in the attainment of your desire (gypsy folklore).

locomotive *see* JOURNEY.

locusts *see* INSECTS.

logs to dream of cleaving logs portends a visit from strangers (Artemidorus).

looking to dream of looking from high places, out of windows, or in a well denotes ambition, imagination and confused desires.

looking glass dreaming of looking in a looking glass or mirror, to married people signifies children. To the young looking in a mirror denotes sweethearts or is an expression of vanity. To see oneself in water forecasts the dreamer's death or that of a friend (Artemidorus). This dream can be directly traced through ancestral memory back to the legends of mythology.

losing dreams of losing things may reflect some sense of loss that the dreamer is feeling; for example, childhood may be now a thing of the past, or a love affair may be over.

In some cases the dream may indicate that a good opportunity may be, or already has been, missed.

loss for a woman to dream of losing her *wedding-ring* denotes little love for her husband. If she finds it again, the love is not wholly dead. For a man to lose his *shoes*, signifies reproaches (gypsy folklore).

lost dreaming of being lost indicates a certain sense of confusion in the dreamer's mind, a lack of direction in life, or mixed feelings towards a particular person or situation.

love all emotions that are felt in dreams are genuine emotions. What has to be decided is whether the love that is felt in the dream is a compensation for that which is deficient in waking life, i.e. wish-fulfilment or a reflection of something that the dreamer feels in waking life yet has not acknowledged. To dream of unsuccessful love is a dream of CONTRARY MEANING, you will marry and be happy. To dream that friends love you foretells prosperity in all things. To dream of being with your lover foretells a speedy marriage (Raphael).

lucky to dream that you are lucky is a dream of CONTRARY MEANING, of misfortune (Raphael).

luggage luggage in dreams may be interpreted as 'emotional baggage', i.e. thoughts and feelings that the dreamer carries about and cannot, or will not, let go of.

lute delightful company, happiness, success (gypsy folklore).

lying to dream of lying is bad except for players and those who practice it professionally (gypsy folklore).

   A dream of lying may be spurred by a dishonest action, or one which is out of character in waking life.

lying down *see* ACTIONS.

lying in bed *see* FURNITURE.

lynx *see* ANIMALS.

M

mace to dream of mace is good, for mace comforts the heart (Artemidorus).

machine machines can be interpreted as that which drives the individual, both in a physical sense (the heart, brain, hormones, etc) and also in a psychological sense (the wishes, desires and emotions which motivate the individual).

maggots *see* INSECTS.

magician a dream predicting unexpected events, surprises (gypsy folklore).

magnet a dream warning you to resist the snares that are across your path. To see a magnet denotes that you are planning to fascinate some other person (Raphael).

magpie *see* BIRDS.

malice to dream that someone bears you malice denotes a sudden advancement to an important position (gypsy folklore).

mallows to dream of eating mallows signifies exemption from trouble, as this herb soothes skin and digestive irritations (Artemidorus). This is an unusually clear example of the folklore from which symbols and symbolism in dreams have been derived.

mantle *see* CLOAK.

map to dream of examining a map denotes that you will leave your native land (gypsy folklore).

maple a dream of comfort and a happy life (gypsy folklore). The national emblem of Canada, indicating goodness, service, etc.

mare *see* ANIMALS.

marigolds these are the symbol of the constant lover, happy marriage, advancement, and riches (Raphael). It is called the flower of flame or light, and is also used to break the spells of enchantment.

mariner a dream denoting voyages (gypsy folklore).

market *see* FAIR.

marriage a dream invariably auguring sickness, death, etc. In the case of a single person, a dream of marriage may be wish-fulfilment, but it can also be an exploration of one's feelings towards marriage, or a safe experiment with the concept.

Symbolically, marriage may represent the 'marriage' of two different, yet coexistent, parts of the self, such as the conscious and the unconscious, or the impulsive and the considerate. It could also mean the marriage between two personality attributes, such as gentleness and courage.

Mars an unfortunate dream forecasting quarrels at home and abroad (gypsy folklore).

marsh to dream of walking in a marshy country signifies a troubled life. SWAMPS denote sorrows and difficulties. To escape them, future comfort. A dream of trying to plough a marsh denotes misery in spite of work (gypsy folklore).

martyr a dream of honour and public approbation (gypsy folklore).

mask a mask is the face that the dreamer presents to the world; the secret or undiscovered aspects of his personality hide behind this.

A mask can also be a face that the individual adopts when coping with certain situations; thus, a soldier in battle will adopt the warrior mask. This is not his 'everyday' face, but, given the situation that is being faced, a genuine one.

masquerade to attend one is a dream of deceptive pleasure (gypsy folklore).

mastiff *see* ANIMALS.

mat to dream that a door mat has been stolen forecasts that someone will try to enter your house (Raphael).

mattress a mattress may represent feelings of comfort and security or a relaxed approach, either to life in general or to a particular situation. Mattresses can also function in dreams much the same way as beds, in that they may represent the dreamer's life as he or she has created it (the bed he has made to lie on). *See also* FURNITURE.

maypole a dream denoting love and lovers (gypsy folklore) The maypole dance and festival had its origin in pagan sex-worship and Freudians would still regard it to be an erotic symbol.

meadow to dream of walking through pleasant meadows portends happiness (gypsy folklore).

medal to dream of receiving medals for good conduct denotes depravity and loss of character (Raphael). This may be a wish dream arising from having a guilty conscience.

medicine to dream of taking it with difficulty is a dream of physical distress.

melon *see* FRUIT.

memory given that we spend so much time dreaming every night, it must be accepted that the great majority of our dreams are forgotten. This is not due to any failure on our part. A combination of circumstances conspires to erase most dreams from our minds. If time has passed between dreaming and waking, the mind may not be sufficiently focused to remember it. Some dreams are confusing and, therefore, difficult to recall with any degree of accuracy. Some dreams are simply too disturbing for the dreamer to confront in waking life and are consequently repressed by the subconscious.

menstruation a man who dreams of menstruation may be exploring his more creative and productive aspects.

A woman who has ceased to menstruate but who dreams of menstruation may be having difficulties coming to terms with ageing and loss of fertility. *See also* BODY; WOUND.

mice *see* ANIMALS.

midwife a dream denoting the revelation of secrets.

milk to drink milk in a dream denotes joy. To sell it, is a prediction of disappointment in love. To dream of milking a cow predicts abundance and good fortune (gypsy folklore).

A sexual interpretation of a dream about milk is that the milk represents semen and that it reflects the sexual desire of the male dreamer. Milk can also reflect a subconscious desire to return to the breast of the mother, or to another important female figure in the dreamer's life.

mill or **miller** a dream that denotes happiness and riches (gypsy folklore).

mirror *see* LOOKING GLASS.

miser like all dreams pertaining to money or hoards, this is unfavourable (gypsy folklore).

mistletoe a dream of fortune and health (gypsy folklore). The legends attached to the plant justify this symbolism.

money money represents things that the dreamer regards as valuable. It can also symbolize power and sex.

monk *see* ABBOT.

monkeys *see* ANIMALS.

monster a monster almost always represents FEAR in a dream. This may be fear the dreamer has of something within him or herself, such as an obsession or an overriding passion, or it may be fear of something that one does not understand properly, such as love or death. *See also* GIANT; OGRE.

moon the moon may represent that which the dreamer believes to be unattainable, or a desire for romance. The many characteristics of the moon are said to have the following mystic interpretations:

a brilliant moon this dream is said to predict love and good health to a wife, to a husband, increase in wealth.

a new moon advancement in business.

waning predicts the death of a great man.

a halo around the moon denotes pardon and deliverance through a female.

a red moon this dream predicts imminent voyages and pilgrimages.

a dull moon this predicts death or illness to wife, sister or female relative. It may also foretell perilous journeys, especially by sea, brain fever or eye trouble.

an obscure moon becoming bright is a prediction of profit to a woman and joy to a man. If the moon goes from *clearness to obscurity*, loss, sadness and misfortune are predicted.

two moons denote increase in rank and dignity.

When a beautiful woman dreams of the moon, the dream forecasts high standing, dignity and admiration. To thieves, murderers, etc, it denotes justice. To invalids it denotes danger of death or shipwreck. For a young girl or widow to dream of a full, dazzling moon, the prognostication is marriage; to a married woman it predicts the birth of a beautiful daughter and to a man it signifies the birth of a son.

morning glory a hopeful, happy dream (gypsy folklore). A symbol of the resurrection (Smith).

mosquitoes *see* INSECTS.

moss a dream signifying the acquisition and hoarding of money (gypsy folklore).

mother to dream of your mother (living) denotes joy; if she is dead, sorrow (gypsy folklore). *See also* TYPICAL DREAMS.

moths *see* INSECTS.

mountain mountains can be construed as obstacles in one's path, difficulties that loom large ahead. A dream of heaviness, fear and trouble (Artemidorus). *See also* TYPICAL DREAMS.

mouse *see* ANIMALS.

mouth *see* BODY.

mud dreams of mud, accompanied by feelings of repulsion, suggest guilt feelings on the part of the dreamer, or a deep-seated belief that something is 'dirty' in sexual terms. Feeling 'soiled' by mud in a dream may suggest that the dreamer is suffering from depression, while dreaming of sinking in mud or QUICK-SAND might suggest suppressed feelings of powerlessness or despair in the dreamer's waking life.

To dream of being covered with mud denotes slander (gypsy folklore). *See also* DIGGING; EXCREMENT; QUAGMIRE.

mulberry-tree a dream of increase of wealth, of abundance of goods (Artemidorus). A symbol of prosperity in Persia and Italy.

mule *see* ANIMALS.

murder committing murder, or desiring to commit murder, in a dream points to the expression in dream life of strong feelings that are repressed in waking life. This is often sexual desire but may also be emotions that the dreamer is unable to express satisfactorily. *See also* TYPICAL DREAMS.

mushrooms to dream of eating them denotes danger of death or personal sickness to the dreamer (gypsy folklore). Evidently an anxiety dream, expressed in the doubt of the mushrooms.

music the playing of music in a dream suggests self-expression. Thus, the person who dreams that he or she can suddenly play beautiful music on an instrument may be fulfilling a waking desire to be able to give vent to certain feelings or to use his or her creative talents.

A dream of ravishing music signifies sudden and delightful news. Harsh sounds denote the contrary (Artemidorus).

N

naked a dream of sickness, poverty, affront, fatigue. Invariably ominous according to older interpreters. Modern students, however, attribute to it a totally different significance; holding it in some instances as a wish dream, in others as an erotic dream and again as a dream symbolizing freedom from social restraint. The theory of the subconscious and its warnings, etc, is, however, in accord with the older school, for the dream of nakedness might readily originate in fear, especially with women who habitually devote a large amount of thought to clothes. *See also* TYPICAL DREAMS.

neck a dream of power, honour, riches. Imperfections or ailments of the neck, however, predict sickness (Artemidorus).

necklace a dream of riches and honour. If you break the necklace it predicts misfortune (gypsy folklore).

nectar a dream of drinking nectar predicts riches, honour and a long life (gypsy folklore). Nectar was the drink of the ancient gods and this is the source of the symbolism.

need a dream of need denotes wealth in store (gypsy folklore). The shrewd interpreter might easily infer that the anxiety that roused the dream would give birth to the frugality or thrift that tend to accumulate wealth.

needles a dream of disputes and quarrels (gypsy folklore).

nest if the nest is full of eggs it is a dream predicting profit, domestic happiness or success in love. A nest with broken eggs, or dead birds reflects distress and desolation, and a feeling of failure and hoplessness.

net to dream of being entangled in a net denotes worry and a powerful enemy who is attempting to ensnare you (gypsy folklore).

nettles to dream of stinging yourself denotes striving to attain desire. In youth it predicts love that will risk all.

newspaper to dream of buying and selling newspapers denotes hard work and small profit. To read one indicates deception (gypsy folklore).

night to be suddenly overtaken by night refers to the sudden appearance of an rival. To walk on a dark night denotes grief, disappointment and loss. It is ominous to dream of night-birds, with the exception of the nightingale, which denotes joyful news to the dreamer. If the dreamer is a married woman, she will have children who will be great singers (Artemidorus). It is said that Jenny Lind's mother dreamed of a nightingale. *See also* TIME.

nightgown to dream of wearing a nightgown denotes an honourable career. To dream of tearing the nightgown signifies that you feel that you have commited a hasty action (gypsy folklore).

nightingale *see* NIGHT.

nightmares the content of a nightmare comes second in importance to the fear that the dreamer necessarily feels while having the nightmare. That is to say that any interpretation of the nightmare has to acknowledge first that the fear is genuine and that it will be reflected in some way in the dreamer's waking thoughts. If the source of this fear in waking life can be pinpointed, (fear of death, fear of one's sexuality, etc) then the interpretation of the other elements of the nightmare will be more straightforward.

nine *see* NUMBERS.

nobility to dream of fraternizing with the nobility, signifies social downfall (gypsy folklore).

nose *see* BODY.

numbers numbers in dreams can be meaningful in relation to the person who is dreaming; for example, two may be significant to a person who has two children. Numbers are also imbued with a more general symbolism.

one may mean unity, wholeness, or the self. In some cases it may be a symbol for the phallus, or represent the male.

two can mean balance between two things, a complementary relationship, two alternatives that are open, or two things that are in opposition.

three may symbolize the genitals of the male, the threesome of two parents and child, or the Holy Trinity.

four may stand for stability and the status quo, the four seasons and the four elements being an essential part of the world as we know it to be.

five represents the human body—five fingers, five toes, five senses, the combination of head, arms and legs.

six is associated with balance, and occasionally sex.

seven represents spirituality or something that is sacred.

eight is symbolic of death and rebirth or resurrection.

nine is a symbol of pregnancy.

ten is a symbol of male and female as one.

twelve is a symbol of time or the whole year.

twenty-four is a symbol of the cycle of night and day.

zero may be a symbol for the female.

numbness a dream implying futile labour and discouragement.

nun *see* ABBOT.

nurse a nurse is a symbol of caring, a dream of being tended by a nurse may be compensation for love that is felt to be lacking in waking life. The caring or nurturing may occasionally have sexual significance. To dream of a nurse denotes sickness, sorrow and trouble (gypsy folklore).

nuts if the kernels are well-filled this is a dream of riches, happiness and honours. Shrivelled kernels denote disappointment (gypsy folklore).

nutmeg to dream of eating one is a dream of sickness. To grate one is an indication of victory despite obstacles (gypsy folklore).

nut trees to see nut TREES and to crack and eat their FRUIT signifies riches gathered at great pains. Hidden nuts denote the discovery of treasure (Artemidorus).

O

oar a dream that predicts a long life, riches, happiness (Artemidorus). The symbol of strength, longevity, etc. To dream of losing an oar is said to refer to the death of the dreamer's father, mother or someone to whom he or she looks for protection (gypsy folklore).

oasis an oasis in a dream may symbolize something, particularly an emotion, that has been missing in the dreamer's life and without which he or she feels barren.

oats a dream denoting success, to each after his own desire (gypsy folklore). Agricultural symbols are invariably auspicious.

obelisk a dream of fame and wealth, of honours to be conferred (gypsy folklore).

obscurity to dream that the SUN is obscured denotes damage to the reputation; to dream that the MOON is obscured affects the life in a lesser degree (gypsy folklore).

obstacles obstacles that the dreamer encounters in dream life will be reflected by inhibitions, uncertainties or restrictions in waking life.

Confronting an obstacle in a dream may point to a need for the dreamer to overcome a fear in waking life.

oculist a dream denoting some fault to repair, some evil or injury to confess (gypsy folklore).

ocean the ocean was the ancient symbol of life. In a dream a calm ocean indicates good, a stormy one ill and a smooth ocean denotes accomplishment in love and in life. *See also* WATER.

offerings and vows to the gods signify a desire to return to virtue and divine love (gypsy folklore).

office to be deposed from office is a dream auguring ill, and if the dreamer be sick it presages death (Artemidorus).

ogre dreams of encounters with ogres will often be an expression of the dreamer's attitudes to authority, or perhaps a father figure. *See also* GIANT and MONSTER.

oil dreaming of oil may indicate a need to 'lubricate' a relationship in order to keep it running along smoothly, whether by adopting peacekeeping tactics in a difference of opinion or by suppressing one's own feelings in order to keep things on an even keel.

ointment a dream of illness (gypsy folklore).

old age a dream denoting wisdom (gypsy folklore).

old woman a fortunate dream. To dream of courting and marrying an old woman is also fortunate, but you will also have criticism from some quarters (Artemidorus).

olive *see* FRUIT.

olive tree peace, delight, dignity and the attainment of desire (Artemidorus).

one *see* NUMBERS.

onions dreaming of onions denotes luck both good and bad. To eat onions predicts receiving money, discovery of lost or stolen articles or a faithful but hasty sweetheart. Also attacks from thieves and failure of crops. To gather onions, joyful news, recovery from illness and a speedy removal (Artemidorus).

opal a dream of deceitful security (gypsy folklore). The bad luck attributed to the gem coincides with the interpretation.

oranges *see* FRUIT.

orchards dreaming of orchards in FRUIT denotes abundance. If there are fountains in the orchard this refers to pleasure and great wit. Barren trees in an orchard bear a contrary meaning (Artemidorus).

orchestra an orchestra playing harmoniously is indicative of the elements in the waking life of the dreamer working together to create a satisfying and harmonious whole. More specifically, it can be a sign of a contented relationship with oneself.

organ the sound of a church organ augurs happiness and prosperity (Raphael).

ornament a dream denoting want and extreme poverty as a result of extravagance (Raphael).

ostrich *see* BIRDS.

otter *see* ANIMALS.

oven an oven may represent pregnancy or the womb. It may also represent one's ability to change as one grows and develops.

overboard to fall overboard from a sailing vessel denotes poverty, imprisonment and sickness (Raphael). This is a dream reflecting anxiety.

owl *see* BIRDS.

oxen *see* ANIMALS.

oysters *see* ANIMALS.

oyster shells *see* ANIMALS.

P

packing packing in a dream indicates a desire that the dreamer has for a change of some sort, getting away from old circumstances and emotions, possibly fulfilling a need for freedom. Dreaming that one is having difficulty in making up one's mind what to pack, or finding it hard to close and fasten the suitcase, would therefore indicate that the dreamer is as yet mentally unprepared for the changes that lie in store.

padlock a padlock denotes mysteries to be solved (gypsy folklore). It is also a Christian symbol of silence.

painting a dream of painting a house denotes sickness in the family, but thrift and luck in business. To paint beautiful landscapes denotes poverty and false hopes (gypsy folklore).

palace a good dream foretelling wealth and dignity (gypsy folklore)

pall to dream of a body being borne to the grave foretells that the dreamer will attend a wedding.

palm a dream foretelling success and prosperity. To a married woman it refers to children, to a single woman it is a prediction of marriage (Artemidorus). The palm is the Christian emblem of victory.

palm tree a dream foreshadowing great joy (gypsy folklore). The sacred tree of lower Egypt, also the Tree of Life (Egyptian). The Scriptural symbol for the righteous and godly.

panic panic felt by dreaming will have its origin in something in the dreamer's life that is causing similar feelings that need to be dealt with. *See also* FEAR.

pansy this dream foretells of a constant sweetheart, but also great poverty. The pansy is the emblem of remembrance and kind thought.

panther *see* ANIMALS.

pantomime a dream denoting living among deceitful persons (gypsy folklore).

paper writing paper that has not been written on may represent things that have gone unsaid or feelings that have not been expressed by the dreamer.

Wrapping paper can be construed, in certain contexts, as either the dreamer's protection against the world, or the persona he or she adopts to show to the world. To dream of white paper denotes innocence. If the paper is written on then deception is a possibility. To dream of printed paper denotes good fortune (gypsy folklore).

paradise a good dream to each according to his desire and calling (Raphael).

paralysis dreams of paralysis may be a reflection of the way in which the dreamer is feeling in waking life—unable to function properly, helpless, etc. They may, however, in a semi-wakened state, merely be a subconscious acknowledgement of the fact that while the individual is dreaming, the major muscle groups are rendered inactive. Can be a dream denoting the approach of illness (gypsy folklore).

parcel parcels and packages can be interpreted in a similar fashion to LETTERS. An unopened parcel or package is indicative of feelings yet to be explored or self-knowledge yet to be acquired.

parents parents in dreams rarely represent real parents, rather the male and female aspects of the dreamer's nature, i.e. the man and woman who are within everybody.

A dream of warning, especially if the parents are dead. If you have been foolish their visit is to rebuke and to warn you of danger (Raphael). It may be a dream inspired by a guilty conscience, expressed through the symbolism of the subconsciousness.

park to walk through a park, health and happiness (Raphael). The difference in the symbolism of the park and that of GROVES and FORESTS is due to the difference in the ages to which they belonged respectively, the park being a medieval institution, while the grove dates to denote antiquity.

parrot *see* BIRDS.

partridges *see* BIRDS.

passing bell to dream of hearing the bell that was once rung to announce a passing funeral denotes the illness of the dreamer or of a near relative (Raphael).

past we may dream of people and things from our past in order to try to recreate the way in which we felt at that time, or alternatively, in order to work out unresolved inner conflicts about those times and to express emotions that have been previously repressed.

patches for a woman to dream of patching her husband's or her children's garments is an excellent prediction of wellbeing and riches (Raphael). Frugality and thrift are invariably recorded as happy omens.

path a difficult, narrow, treacherous or winding path will point to troubles in waking life. A smooth, well-trodden path will indicate that the dreamer is adopting a 'safe' approach to life, following in the footsteps of others perhaps.

pawnbroker a dream of poverty, losses and disappointments (gypsy folklore).

peaches *see* FRUIT.

peacock *see* BIRDS.

pearls a dream of tears (gypsy folklore). The jewel is also symbolic of weeping, especially to brides.

pears *see* FRUIT.

peas a dream denoting success in business (Artemidorus).

pen pencil pens and pencils are means of communication. Occasionally, a pen or a pencil may act as a dream metaphor for the male sexual organ.

Dreaming of a pen is said to predict adversity and loss to a business man (gypsy folklore). Probably derived from the idea that knowledge interfered with the accomplishment of business.

penis *see* BODY.

pepper a dream denoting truthfulness to the verge of irritation (gypsy folklore).

performing *see* ACTING.

perfume to compound petals and to distribute perfume among friends is a dream predicting agreeable news. To receive perfume as a gift denotes news in accordance with whether the scent is agreeable or otherwise.

pest or **pestilence** a dream threatening sickness and misfortune (gypsy folklore).

pets dreams of puppies or kittens may not so much reflect a woman's desire to own a cute baby animal as to have a child of her own. To dream of having one denotes protection by friends. *See also* ANIMALS.

petticoat a dream of trouble and sorrow (Raphael).

pheasants *see* BIRDS.

phoenix a dream of renewed health and vigour (gypsy folklore). The symbol of immortality, resurrection, the soul.

photographs photographs are images; a photograph of the past in a dream represents the dreamer's image of the past, while a photo of the dreamer him or herself will represent the dreamer's self-image.

A dream warning you to make a final settlement of your affairs (gypsy folklore).

pickaxe a warning of coming evil, perhaps destruction by fire (gypsy folklore).

pictures a dream of falsehood and deceit (Raphael).

pies to dream of making pies augurs joy and profit (gypsy folklore).

pig *see* ANIMALS.

pigeons *see* BIRDS.

pillow a dream prognosticating death (gypsy folklore). The pillow is a Christian symbol of eternal rest. It was used as a symbol of power and placed with the dead in order to enable them to lift their heads.

pill we take medicine because we believe it is doing us good and not because we like the taste. Similarly, dreaming of swallowing pills would indicate that the dreamer is doing something in waking life not because he or she wishes to do it but because he or she feels it to be necessary, either good for the dreamer, or a good thing to do in a moral sense.

  This is a dream forecasting sickness (gypsy folklore). This interpretation is attributable to sensory stimuli, and to subconscious knowledge of a physical condition.

pilot a dream of a pilot is one of safety and protection (gypsy folklore).

pincers a dream of persecution and injustice (gypsy folklore). In Christian symbolism pincers represent martyrdom.

pineapples *see* FRUIT.

pine cone a happy dream auguring health (gypsy folklore). The pine cone is the symbol of life, abundance and power.

pine tree to see a pine tree in your dream signifies idleness and remissness (Artemidorus). This tree was especially dedicated to Dionysius, hence the interpretation after the passing of the Greek Gods.

pins this dream signifies contradiction and discussion of trivial matters (gypsy folklore). Sharp or pointed instruments usually have an unpleasant interpretation.

pipe a dream of a pipe is one of peace and tranquillity (gypsy folklore). The symbolism of the 'Pipe of Peace' is probably derived from the American Indian.

pirate to be captured by a pirate may symbolize threat and a feeling of loss of control to the dreamer. For a woman it may signify that she thinks her partner has too much control in her life. To a girl this dream predicts marriage to a foreigner; to a man it signifies travel in strange lands (Raphael). *See also* PLANK.

pistol *see* GUN.

pit a dream forecasting the decline of business, possible descent to want and distress. To fall into a pit denotes misfortune and tragedy (Raphael).

pitchfork an evil dream except to farmers, to whom it predicts wealth through toil (gypsy folklore). The pitchfork is a symbol of Satan in Christian art.

pitcher to dream of carrying a pitcher is a dream of failure. To dream of dropping or breaking it predicts disaster, death (gypsy folklore).

place the place in which the dream scenario plays out will do much to reflect the dreamer's state of mind or mood in real life.

planets a dream denoting joyful tidings (gypsy folklore). Probably derived from the Biblical description of the birth of Christ.

plank to walk a plank in your dream forewarns you of treachery (gypsy folklore). *See also* PIRATES.

plants *see* FLOWERS.

ploughing ploughing is generally seen as a symbol of sexual intercourse, the preparing of fertile ground, the sowing of the seed, etc.

plums *see* FRUIT.

pole the most obvious interpretation of a pole or anything similar in shape that appears in a dream is a sexual one, i.e. that the pole represents the male organ.

pole star a dream of loyalty and devotion (gypsy folklore). The universal emblem of stability.

police to a decent person this dream denotes honours (Raphael).

pomegranate *see* FRUIT.

pond *see* BROOK.

poniard a dream featuring this small pointed dagger denotes injustice and persecution (gypsy folklore). A Christian symbol of martyrdom. *See also* WEAPONS.

pool *see* WATER.

popcorn a dream of eating popcorn augurs a pleasant surprise.

poplar to dream of a green poplar denotes fulfilled hopes, if withered it denotes disappointment (gypsy folklore). It was once held sacred to Heracles. Afterwards it symbolized the Holy Rood of the Christians.

poppy a dream denoting illness to the sleeper or tidings of illness to loved ones (gypsy folklore). An interpretation evidently derived from the use of the poppy in the manufacture of opium, rather than from the symbolism of the blossoms.

porcupine *see* ANIMALS.

porpoise a dream of joy and happiness (Artemidorus).

portfolio a dream bespeaking mysteries, things hidden from sight (gypsy folklore).

portrait a dream forecasting long life to the person represented, especially if the portrait is painted on wood. To receive or to give a portrait away signifies treason (gypsy folklore).

position one's position in a dream, in particular in relation to other people in the dream, will be significant in terms of one's position in life, i.e. how one sees oneself in relation to the world, not only to position, but also to time, morality and beliefs.

closeness either stands for intimacy, someone the dreamer feels close to, or an idea or value that he or she holds dear.

distance denotes something from which the dreamer feels remote. This may be an unachievable aim or a set of beliefs from which he or she feels detached.

height dreaming that one is above something or someone, looking down upon them, may indicate the dreamer's feeling of moral or intellectual superiority. It might also mean that the dreamer feels he or she has 'risen above' certain difficulties in life.

Where the individual dreams of being at a lower level, looking up at things or people, these things or people may represent higher ideals to which the dreamer aspires, or, in some contexts, an authority, a superior being or a God. *See also* HEIGHT.

in front/behind generally speaking, things that lie behind the dreamer may be interpreted as things or ideas of the past which have now been left behind. What lies in front of the dreamer is, therefore, the future.

potatoes to dream of digging potatoes predicts success and profit. If, however, there are only a few or they are very small, this denotes failure (gypsy folklore).

poultice to dream that one is applied to any part of the body implies trouble to that particular organ or limb (gypsy folklore).

poverty a dream of CONTRARY MEANING to the poor, but ill for the rich or for those who use eloquent speech (Artemidorus).

precipice dreaming of standing at the top of a precipice suggests fear of 'taking the plunge', i.e. fear of failure.

Falling off the edge of a precipice may be either a feeling of loss of control in waking life, or a symbol of death or what is not understood. Being trapped at the bottom of a precipice in a dream would suggest that the dreamer feels helpless and trapped in his or her present situation. *See also* ABYSS; TYPICAL DREAMS.

presents presents in dreams may represent affection in real life. *See also* GIFTS.

priest *see* ABBOT.

primroses a dream boding sickness, sorrow, death (Raphael).

prison a dream of CONTRARY MEANING denoting happiness, hope, etc (Raphael). Evidently many of these interpretations trace their derivation to the days of the early Christians when persecution and humiliation were borne with joy and hope. *See also* IMPRISONMENT.

prize dreaming of receiving a prize may indicate a wish for recognition in the waking life of the dreamer.

procession to see one in a dream denotes happiness and joy to come (gypsy folklore).

profanation misery and future misfortune are herein denoted (gypsy folklore).

prostitution dreams of prostitution are generally indicative of some sexual need. A man who dreams of being with a prostitute may be seeking pure sexual gratification, without the need for emotional attachment. If the feeling of the dream is one of disgust, the man may want to express some aspect of his sexuality about which he feels ashamed.

Women who dream of prostitution may feel guilty about sex, or may have sexual needs that are not being met because they are being repressed.

prunes *see* FRUIT.

public house to dream of keeping a public house denotes extremes financially. To dream of drinking in one denotes sickness, poverty or imprisonment for debt (gypsy folklore).

puddles a dream denoting undesirable acquaintances who will get the dreamer into trouble (gypsy folklore).

pumpkin to dream of a pumpkin predicts that the dreamer will have admirers. To eat one signifies indisposition (gypsy folklore).

punishment the person who dreams of dire punishments and retribution may well suffer from attacks of conscience in waking life, especially if his or her way of life is at odds with the set of morals he or she was brought up with.

purity of the air the dream of pure air is supposedly lucky. Of a dream of bad air, the reverse may be said (gypsy folklore).

purse the purse is a symbol of the female genitalia. The interpretation of a dream of one will depend very much on how it is viewed by the dreamer. This dream may express feelings concerning loss of femininity or anxiety over possible infertility or the approach of the menopause.

To find a full purse is said to be a prediction of happiness; to dream of losing one denotes sickness (gypsy folklore).

pyramid a dream of grandeur and wealth. To be on top of one predicts great achievement (gypsy folklore).

Q

quagmire to fall into one predicts impassable barriers (Artemidorus). *See also* MUD and QUICKSAND.

quail *see* BIRDS.

quarrel dreams about quarrelling or fighting mostly indicate that the dreamer is going through an inner struggle of some kind.

The mystical view is that this is a dream of the contrary, to quarrel in a dream means to make love (Raphael).

quarry to dream of falling down a quarry denotes sudden illness (gypsy folklore).

quay a dream that promises protection (gypsy folklore).

quayside departures from a quayside are indicative of change in the life of the dreamer. One who dreams of taking leave at a quayside will very possibly be embarking on a significantly different stage in life.

Farewells at the quayside are acknowledgements of old ways and of thoughts being left behind. *See also* JOURNEY.

queen to behold a king or a queen in a dream predicts joy, honour and prosperity (Artemidorus).

question to ask questions in a dream signifies good luck. If the dreamer is asked questions he or she is unable to answer, then this this signifies ill fortune.

quicksands a dream warning you of temptations and weaknesses of which you are unaware (Raphael). *See also* MUD; QUAGMIRE.

quicksilver a dream denoting changes, vicissitudes and restlessness (gypsy folklore).

R

rabbit *see* ANIMALS.

racoon *see* ANIMALS.

race dreaming of taking part in a race suggests a sense of competitiveness, an awareness of one's position in life and, depending on the dream, either acknowledgement that one might not succeed or a sense of achievement at this particular stage in life. Sometimes a race might indicate a particular rivalry in the dreamer's life.

A good dream to well persons, to the sick a speedy termination to the race of life is denoted (Artemidorus).

radio this is generally a symbol for communication or, in some cases, intuition, i.e. an ability to pick up feelings 'in the air'.

rags a dream of CONTRARY MEANING predicting success (gypsy folklore).

raffle a dream of doubt and uncertainty (gypsy folklore).

raft a warning of danger from which you will be delivered (gypsy folklore).

railway a dream that is generally symbolic of the dreamer's journey through life, denoting change (gypsy folklore). *See also* JOURNEY and PATH.

rain dreams of torrential rain may point to feelings of depression or may indicate a cleansing process of some sort, i.e. a 'washing away' of guilt feelings or sadness, or a flood of long-repressed emotion.

    The rain may have a refreshing quality to it and therefore represent some much needed change in the dreamer's life or spiritual wellbeing.

    Rain is said to predict trouble, heavy, or not, according to state of the rain in the dream (Raphael). *See also* DELUGE.

rainbow in general this is a good sign for the future, or a sign denoting a change in the dreamer's present condition. A rainbow in the East denotes benefits to the poor and the sick. In the West it is a good omen for the rich but not for the poor. A rainbow overhead denotes a change in fortune, although this might mean a change for the worse. A rainbow on the right is a good sign, on the left, bad, judging right and left according to the sun. Wherever it appears it is thought to bring good fortune to those who are in poverty and suffering affliction by changing the air (Artemidorus).

raking a dream of success (Raphael).

ram *see* ANIMALS.

rape dreams of rape do not necessarily point to a fear of being raped (or of raping), nor do they point to desires on the dreamer's part. Rape is essentially violence, intrusion and abuse of power; dreams of rape are more likely to be exploring the dreamer's feelings in relation to these concepts rather than in relation to the rape itself.

raspberries *see* FRUIT.

rats *see* ANIMALS.

raven *see* BIRDS.

reading to dream of reading romance indicates joy; to dream of reading serious books, wisdom (Artemidorus).

recurring dreams it is quite common for people to begin having a certain dream fairly early on in life and then to continue having dreams that, even if they are not the same, are very similar in many ways, several times over a period of many years. The recurrence of dreams points to the recurrence of certain sorts of situations or emotions in the dreamer's waking life. The dreamer's reaction to, or way of coping with, the situation or emotion has altered little over the years and so the dream relating to the situation or emotion has remained, in essence, the same. When the dreamer matures or changes and ceases to react in this way then the dream will no longer occur or will be very different.

red *see* COLOURS.

reeds to dream of seeing them near the WATER warns you to be decisive if you want to succeed (gypsy folklore). The scriptural metaphor uses them to symbolize weakness.

reflection you see yourself in a reflection, and so a reflection in a dream is the view that the dreamer holds of him or herself, i.e. it is his or her own self-image.

reindeer *see* ANIMALS.

relics this dream comes as a warning to guard your valuables (gypsy folklore).

religion any individual, whether religious or not, may dream of religious figures or religious imagery. The appearance of a religious figure, of God even, need not be related to religion in any way. For example, God may represent a figure of authority whom the dreamer respects deeply. Religious imagery may merely indicate that the dreamer needs to turn inwards more and to get in touch with the spiritual side of him or herself. *See also* GOD.

reptile a reptile is a symbol of anger, quarrels and bitterness. If a single woman has this dream it denotes a false lover.

rescue a dream forecasting a rise in the world, and the possible establishment of a successful business (gypsy folklore).

revenge to dream of taking revenge predicts a bed of sickness for the dreamer (Raphael).

rice to dream of eating rice denotes abundance of instruction (Artemidorus). Certain legends and traditions of Western Europe associate rice with wisdom because sages were said to live upon it, such as the yogis of India, etc.

riches a dream of CONTRARY MEANING (gypsy folklore).

riding a dream of good fortune (Raphael). A dream of a galloping horse is an erotic one (Freud, Jung).

ring for a woman to dream that her wedding ring breaks denotes the death of her husband. If the ring presses her finger the dream forecasts the illness of her husband or of someone in his family. To dream that someone draws a ring on the dreamer's finger denotes marriage (Raphael). In all times the ring has been held as an amulet of affection and of home, its suggestion in a dream is therefore obvious. *See also* LOSS.

river to see a broad, rapid and muddy river is a dream denoting difficulties. Calm and clear water predicts happiness and prosperity (Raphael). The river is usually taken as a symbol of human life and represented as smooth or turbulent according to the nature of the occurrences. *See also* WATER.

road *see* PATH.

robin *see* BIRDS.

rock a rock may represent stability, 'down-to-earthness', or simply what is real. Rocks are symbols of impassable obstacles (gypsy folklore).

rocket to dream of a rocket denotes a momentary triumph. The symbolism here may well have been derived from the old proverb of 'going up like a rocket and coming down like a stick.' *See also* TORPEDO.

rod a dream of sadness (gypsy folklore). Dreaming of a rod or any other similar object may have significance as an erotic symbol, denoting the penis (Freud).

roof a dream indicating command and dignity (gypsy folklore).

rook *see* BIRDS.

root To dream of eating them denotes mental disorder (gypsy folklore).

rope depending upon the context of the dream, a rope may represent the umbilical cord, one's attachment to someone close, e.g. one's mother, or it may represent a restriction to the dreamer or the dreamer's own inhibitions in waking life. To dream of being led by ropes warns you against making any contracts with others (gypsy folklore).

rosemary to see it in a dream is a good sign. To smell it, however, is an augury of death (gypsy folklore).

roses in season this is a dream of happiness; dead, wilted, or out of season a dream of trouble and poverty (gypsy folklore).

rouge a dream of treason and deceit (Raphael).

rowing a dream of success unless the boat is upset, in which case it is bad (Raphael).

ruins a dream of CONTRARY MEANING denoting unexpected gains (gypsy folklore).

running *see* ACTIONS.

running sore *see* ABSCESS.

rust dreaming of rust is an indication of destruction of property (gypsy folklore).

rye to see it growing is a dream of triumph over enemies.

S

sable to be in a room hung with sable is a dream which was said to predict the death of a close friend (Artemidorus).

saber a dream of triumph over enemies (gypsy folklore). An erotic dream (Freud). *See also* WEAPONS.

sack a sack or bag is most commonly a symbol for the womb in a dream.

sage to dream of the herb sage is a prediction of honour and advancement (Raphael).

sailboat *see* BOAT.

sailing *see* JOURNEY.

sailor a sailor warns of a dangerous sea voyage (Raphael).

salamander *see* ANIMALS.

salmon *see* ANIMALS.

salt salt is what gives the dreamer's life its flavour, the dreamer's attitudes to situations encountered, the feelings sparked off through interaction with others, the influence and moods of those who surround the dreamer in daily life. Wisdom is here foretold (gypsy folklore). Salt is the symbol of wisdom and wit.

sand dreams of walking on sand, particularly deep, soft sand or sand dunes, reflect feelings of insecurity on the part of the dreamer.

satin a dream of joy and profit, etc (gypsy folklore).

satyr a dream of lechery and lewdness (gypsy folklore).

scaffold *see* GALLOWS.

scarecrow a dream denoting dishonest friends (gypsy folklore).

school in dreams, school represents the values and restrictions that we impose on our own lives as a result of early experience.

To dream of attending school and being unable to learn shows an undertaking that the dreamer does not understand (Artemidorus). *See also* EXAMS; TYPICAL DREAMS.

scissors a dream forecasting marriage for a young girl, but it is a bad omen for a married woman (gypsy folklore). An erotic dream (Jung).

scorpions *see* ANIMALS.

scratch a dream forecasting an accident (gypsy folklore).

scroll this dream forecasts the revelation of secret things (gypsy folklore).

scythe the loss of a friend through death (gypsy folklore). The scythe was the medieval emblem of death.

sea placid and smooth denotes happiness; rough and turbulent, sorrow (gypsy folklore). *See also* WATER.

searching dreams of searching might indicate some feeling of loss in waking life, a loved one, perhaps, or one's childhood. Alternatively, it can indicate a search for a new path in life, that is, a new start. To dream of searching, but not finding, may show either that what is lost is lost forever or that the dreamer has some apprehension about finding what he or she is looking for.

seed seeds may simply represent parts of the human reproductive process, the sperm or egg. Alternatively, much like acorns, seeds can symbolize potential, either in people or situations.

To sow seed in a dream is said to predict the foundation of future wealth, joy, and health (gypsy folklore).

seeing seeing is the sense that all sighted people predominantly use in their dreams, although their eyes are not functioning as they do in waking life.

The imagery and impressions that a dream leaves us with are translated into their sensory equivalents, and sight is the most common of these. Thus, our dreams offer us a panorama through which we can gain greater insight into aspects of our lives and our inner selves. Seeing things in dreams will offer the chance for the dreamer to see him or herself in a clearer light in real life.

sentinel a dream of personal security (gypsy folklore).

seraglio feebleness of disposition and inactivity are here indicated (gypsy folklore).

seraphim a dream of spiritual exaltation, piety (gypsy folklore).

serpent a dream of temptation and of evil (gypsy folklore). Obviously the dream interpreters of modern times have accepted the Christian and Jewish symbolism, rather than that of more remote antiquity. Freud and Jung, however, revert to more primitive times and interpret this as an erotic dream. Raphael interprets the serpent dream as one of 'a deadly enemy bent on your ruin; to kill one denotes success over your enemy'. The serpent was the ancient Egyptian symbol of wisdom and of the sun. Curled in a circle it represented time without end; twisted around a staff, it denoted health. 'More subtle thou art than any beast of the field.' (Bible). *see also* REPTILE; SNAKE.

servants to dream of having servants symbolizes having secret enemies. To hear them talk denotes scandal and suspicion (gypsy folklore).

seven *see* NUMBERS.

sex sex is a basic force that drives all humans. The human race needs to procreate in order to survive. Being a basic, primitive urge, it has come, through time, to be seen as somehow 'at odds' with the rational side of human beings. Animals are primitive, human beings have reasoning. Consequently, humans have imposed upon themselves certain restraints concerning sexual behaviour. These restraints are not universally the same, and it is true to say that for many people, their conditioning concerning sexual behaviour through family, religious authority, etc, may be completely at odds with his or her desires. Thus, sexual desires have to be sublimated in waking life.

The dream world is a safe place for the dreamer to explore feelings that he or she may feel prevented from expressing in waking life. Thus it can act as a release for sexual tension. Dreams of sex, or dreams in which sexual symbols occur (and there are many), can, if interpreted properly, offer considerable insight to the dreamer.

It must be added, however, that overtly sexual dreams can disturb some people and fill them with such feelings of guilt and revulsion that they try to sublimate the dreams themselves, instead of using the dream as a simple release or tool for building greater self-awareness.

shamrock the shamrock denotes good health and longevity, some say a journey by water (gypsy folklore).

shark *see* ANIMALS.

sheaves a favourable dream (gypsy folklore).

sheep *see* ANIMALS.

shellfish *see* ANIMALS.

shelter to dream of seeking shelter against rain denotes secret trouble. To fly from a storm indicates evil to come; to find shelter predicts misery and despair. To have shelter refused predicts eventual triumph and joy (gypsy folklore). Here the interpretation is easily traceable to early Christian persecution, when shelter and food were refused to the elect.

shepherd to dream of being a shepherd is a dream denoting great piety and charity (gypsy folklore). Jesus Christ was called the 'Good Shepherd' giving the symbolism here.

ship a dream of hopes and plans, fulfilled according to the fate of the dreamer in question (gypsy folklore). Also the Christian symbol of hope, etc. *See also* BOAT and JOURNEY.

shipwreck a shipwreck is a symbol of abandoned hopes and misfortunes. To see others shipwrecked in your dream denotes that you will rise above them (gypsy folklore).

shirt a torn shirt denotes slander; to tear it yourself is a symbol of indiscretion. A whole and good shirt is a dream of success (gypsy folklore).

shoemaker to dream of a shoemaker predicts a life of toil and difficulty (gypsy folklore).

shoes to dream of wearing a new pair of shoes denotes many JOURNEYS. To travel without shoes means comfort and honour as you pass through life (Raphael). *See also* LOSS.

shooting a shooting in a dream may be a metaphor for sexual assault. To shoot a bird augurs completion of purpose; to shoot and miss is ominous. To shoot a bird of prey forecasts triumph over enemies (Raphael). *See also* KILLING and WEAPONS.

shower *see* RAIN.

shrimp *see* ANIMALS.

shrinking dreaming of shrinking is perhaps an expression of feelings of insignificance or humility.

shrubs love and happiness are augured by this dream (gypsy folklore).

sibyl to consult a sibyl denotes deception and ill-founded fears; to dream of being one forecasts the disclosure of future events (gypsy folklore).

sickness to dream of being sick denotes illness or imprisonment. To dream of attending the sick denotes joy and virtue.

sieve a dream of waste and want (gypsy folklore).

silk to be clad in silk predicts honour. To dream of trading in silk is a prediction of profit (Artemidorus).

silver a dream auguring unsuspected revelation (gypsy folklore). Silver is the emblem of knowledge.

singing this is a dream of CONTRARY MEANING that it is a dream of lamentation. To sing yourself signifies your own trouble, to hear others sing denotes distress among friends (Raphael).

sinking *see* WATER.

Siren domestic difficulties are denoted by a dream of the mythological sea nymphs the Sirens (gypsy folklore). The symbolism is derived from the Greek myth that the singing of the Sirens lured sailors to their deaths on the rocks they inhabited.

six *see* NUMBERS.

skeleton a dream of horror and fright (gypsy folklore). *See also* FEAR.

skull a dream denoting penance (gypsy folklore). Here the symbolism is obviously Christian.

sky to see the sky clear and blue denotes health and prosperity; cloudy, troubles in proportion to the clouds (gypsy folklore).

slang to use slang in a dream augurs pleasure followed by regret (gypsy folklore).

slave to dream of seeing a slave punished denotes arbitrary injustice of which you will be the victim (gypsy folklore).

sliding a dream of success. To fall, however, connotes misfortune. To be tripped denotes an enemy (Raphael). *See also* TYPICAL DREAMS.

smoke a dream indicating false glory (gypsy folklore).

snail *see* ANIMALS.

snake *see* SERPENT and ANIMALS.

snow a dream of prosperity. A snow storm, however, foretells difficulties from which the dreamer will escape (gypsy folklore).

soap a dream of transient worries (gypsy folklore).

soldiers a soldier may be an expression of the discipline, or lack of it, in the dreamer's life. Abandonment of present employment is predicted in this dream.

sovereign to dream that you are a sovereign is a dream of CONTRARY MEANING indicating disgrace (gypsy folklore).

spade to dream of a spade is a dream signifying futile toil (gypsy folklore).

sparrows *see* BIRDS.

spear a dream of suffering at the hands of enemies (gypsy). A symbol of the Passion, the spear was also worshipped as the emblem of the god Mars. Freud attributes an erotic meaning to this dream. *See also* WEAPONS.

spectacles to dream of wearing them denotes disgrace and low spirits (gypsy folklore).

spice a sad dream (gypsy folklore). A symbol of the passion and death of Christ.

spiders *see* ANIMALS.

spinning this dream denotes many worries.

spools of thread a dream of serious worries (gypsy folklore).

spring good fortune and success (gypsy folklore).

staff a dream of pilgrimage and journeys (gypsy folklore). Dreaming of a staff may also have a sexual significance.

stag *see* ANIMALS.

stars *see* PLANETS.

starving a dream of CONTRARY MEANING auguring success and plenty (gypsy folklore).

steps to walk up steps is a dream auguring success in love, a happy marriage and a rise in life (Raphael).

stiffness someone who dreams of feeling stiff or being unable to move with any flexibility may, in waking life, be taking an attitude of inflexibleness about some situation.

sting a dream of a sting by a BEE, WASP or HORNET denotes injury by a wicked person (Raphael).

stockings to dream of stockings is a dream of distress and trouble. Holes warn you to guard your conduct (gypsy folklore).

stork *see* BIRDS.

storm heavy misfortunes which will vanish (gypsy folklore).

stranger to see a stranger is a dream of honour and success.

straw misfortune, lack of money (gypsy folklore).

strawberries *see* FRUIT.

stream *see* BROOK, RIVER and WATER.

struggling with a burglar or in a dangerous place is a dream of the attainment of honour. The struggle to obtain mastery denotes recovery from illness, to dream of being overcome in a struggle forecasts that the subject may be near to death (gypsy folklore).

success a dream of CONTRARY MEANING signifying failure (gypsy folklore).

sugar to dream of swallowing a quantity of sugar denotes that privation is about to beset you (gypsy folklore).

suicide a dream denoting misfortunes brought about by yourself (gypsy folklore). It is not a prediction of your own oncoming death but, as with many dreams of death, it signifies a change, this time in the way that you lead you life.

sulphur a dream of purification (gypsy folklore). Medieval physicians thought sulphur the greatest disinfectant and purifier.

sun to see the sun is a dream of success. The sun rising denotes good news. A setting sun is bad, while for the sun to be overcast foretells troubles and changes (gypsy folklore). The sun is the invariable symbol of light and wisdom, and can represent warm feelings about something or towards someone.

sundial a dream denoting wasted time (gypsy folklore).

surroundings the surroundings in which a dream is seen to be played out are often reflections of the dreamer's feelings. Thus, a sombre and dreary setting is likely to indicate depressed feelings on the dreamer's part, while bright colours will reflect feelings of happiness and contentment. A dream of cold surroundings, with snow and ice perhaps, can reflect emotional or attitudinal coldness, and a dream of a warm, safe environment will indicate that the dreamer feels secure and content.

swallow *see* BIRDS.

swamp to dream of getting into a swamp foretells vexations through lack of money. *See also* MARSH.

swan *see* BIRDS.

sweetheart to dream that he or she is well and smiling denotes purity and constancy. If your sweetheart is pale or ailing, the reverse is the case (Raphael).

swimming with the head above water, success; the head under water, denotes misfortune; to sink forecasts ruin (Raphael). *See also* TYPICAL DREAMS.

sword to wear one is a dream denoting authority; to be cut with one, humiliation (gypsy folklore). *See also* WEAPONS.

sycamore this dream signifies marriage to a single person, but jealousy to the wedded (gypsy folklore). In Eastern lands it symbolized the tree of life.

T

table to see one denotes sensual pleasures, to break one in your dream predicts a removal (gypsy folklore).

tablet a dream forecasting amazing events (gypsy folklore).

tack a dream of quarrels and enmity (gypsy folklore).

talking talking in a dream may represent a deeper form of communication than talking in daily life.

Sometimes people dream that they try to talk but cannot manage to get the words out, or find that all they can do is babble meaninglessly. This indicates that the dreamer is unable to express some feeling in waking life, or that he or she feels emotionally cut off from other people, misunderstood and frustrated.

tamarind a dream of this tree denotes rain or news and trouble through a woman (gypsy folklore).

tambourine a dream of good luck (gypsy folklore). The gypsy instrument at festivals.

tar dreaming of tar denotes travels by water. If tar is found on the hands, this denotes a difficulty (gypsy folklore).

tassels a dream denoting delight (gypsy folklore).

tea a dream denoting encumbered finances (gypsy folklore).

teapot augurs new friendships (gypsy folklore).

tears a dream of CONTRARY MEANING denoting joy (gypsy folklore).

teasing to dream of teasing denotes trouble and sickness. To dream of being teased denotes good news (gypsy folklore).

teeth *see* BODY and TYPICAL DREAMS.

telegram you will go on a very long journey after dreaming of a telegram (gypsy folklore).

telephones telephones, and what is done with them in a dream, will reflect the dreamer's feelings about how he or she is able or unable to communicate his or her emotions to other people in waking life.

tempest *see* STORM.

temple *see* CHURCH.

ten *see* NUMBERS.

tent denotes war or a quarrel close at hand (gypsy folklore).

tests dreaming of tests may be a reflection of the dreamer's awareness of being judged by his or her actions in daily life. They may also be general stress-induced anxiety dreams. *See also* EXAMS and TYPICAL DREAMS.

thermometer a dream denoting fever or some sudden change in the temperature (gypsy folklore).

thicket *see* HEDGE.

thighs to dream of their being broken or injured implies an accident or death in a foreign country (gypsy folklore).

thimble a dream denoting a vain search for work (gypsy folklore).

thirst to quench a thirst with clear water denotes sleep and contentment. To drink tepid or foul water is an indication of feelings of discomfort lasting through the night (gypsy folklore).

thistle to mow thistles denotes insolence, to be pricked by one forecasts vexation (gypsy folklore).

thorns a dream denoting grief, care and difficulties (gypsy folklore). Thorns are symbols of the Christian Passion.

thread a dream denoting mysterious intrigues. To unravel the thread denotes the discovery of a secret. A dream of gold thread denotes success through intrigue; silver thread indicates that this intrigue is frustrated (gypsy folklore).

three *see* NUMBERS.

throat *see* BODY; TYPICAL DREAMS.

throne a dream connoting credit, renown and honour (gypsy folklore).

thunder *see* LIGHTNING.

tide to watch the tide is a dream of sorrow (gypsy folklore). *See also* WATER.

tiger *see* ANIMALS.

time time can do strange things in dreams. We can find ourselves as an adult among the people and places of our childhood, and we can leap from one apparent time zone to another without disturbing the continuity of the dream. Certain times of day, however, are thought to have certain meanings within the world of dreams.

afternoon/evening may represent the later years of life.

daylight/daytime may represent the conscious self.

morning may represent childhood.

night its blackness may represent that which is unknown, perhaps that which lies in the future. According to the mood of the dream, night may represent a time of fear, or a time of peace and rest.

tinker a dream denoting trouble with neighbours (gypsy folklore).

toad *see* ANIMALS.

toadstool a dream denoting sudden elevation (gypsy folklore). Interpretation derived from their growth of a single night.

tobacco a dream denoting sensual pleasure (gypsy folklore).

toil dreaming of toil, rude labour, drawing water, etc, denotes servitude to the rich and profit to the poor (gypsy folklore).

tomato to dream of eating a tomato denotes happiness of a short duration (gypsy folklore). For many years the tomato was thought to be poisonous and was considered dangerous to eat.

tomb a dream of marriage, the more handsome the tomb the more brilliant the alliance (gypsy folklore).

tools tools can often be interpreted as representing the male sexual organ in dreams. In certain contexts, when a tool is being used as a weapon, this may indicate hidden feelings of aggression, perhaps of a sexual nature.

torches *see* FIRE, CANDLES etc.

torpedo a dream foretelling a shocking discovery (gypsy folklore). The obvious Freudian interpretation of a torpedo in a dream is that it is a phallic symbol. *See also* ROCKET.

torrent to wade in one, sorrows, adversity; to be caught in one, danger of lawsuits (gypsy folklore).

tortoise *see* ANIMALS.

touching touching can indicate satisfactory communication with others. Feeling oneself being touched may represent conscious awareness. Trying not to touch or be touched by somebody may indicate anger and perhaps a desire to detach oneself from him or her.

tower most obviously, a tower in a dream may have a phallic meaning; alternatively, it can reflect feelings of aloofness or of isolation. To ascend a tower signifies a reversal of fortune (gypsy folklore). Interpretation corresponds with the aversion of the Hebrews for towers, an example of which is instanced in the story of the Tower of Babel.

train journey *see* JOURNEY.

train, missing a *see* TYPICAL DREAMS.

trap a dream of losses through law and lawsuits (gypsy folklore).

trap door to see someone emerging from a trap door is a dream of a secret divulged. To dream of one shut down denotes mystery and hidden treasures (gypsy folklore).

travelling *see* JOURNEY.

treasure *see* JEWELS.

tree the tree can be understood to represent all aspects of our life. It is a manifestation of our growth and of where we are coming from. The roots represent our roots, and the branches represent the different aspects of our personalities and our direction in life. Its buds and new leaves represent new life; both that of future generations, and new life in the sense of spiritual renewal. *Falling leaves* are symbolic of that which is cast off from us, the things that we leave behind as we progress through life. The FRUIT of the tree stands for what we have created in life; our achievements, our children and our own selves can all be seen as our 'fruit'. The flowers of the tree may be seen as the human ability to procreate, or more specifically, female fertility. The bark is our protectiveness towards ourselves. The growth of the tree is a mirror for the growth of our bodies and spirits, and for the energy or life force that is necessary for that growth.

A dead tree seen in a dream may represent the death of a person, or the passing of something in your life. *See also* FLOWER, FRUIT.

trench a dream denoting siege and triumph over resistance.

triangle a dream concerning objects of respect and adoration (gypsy folklore).

tripod a dream of unveiling the future, of uncertainty (gypsy folklore). Obviously derived from the tripod upon which the oracles were seated when forecasting.

trout *see* ANIMALS.

trumpet to blow a trumpet denotes triumph over enemies. To hear one denotes coming trouble (Raphael). Invariably the symbol of triumph.

trunk if the trunk is full it shows economy. If it is empty it denotes extravagance (Raphael).

tub always a bad dream. If the tub is filled with water it denotes evil. If it is empty it predicts misfortune (Raphael).

tumble *see* FALLING.

tunnel to dream of crawling through a tunnel may indicate a subconscious wish for 'rebirth' of some sort, i.e. a fresh start. This tunnel symbolizes the birth canal.

A tunnel may also, in certain contexts, be interpreted as a passageway or a positive route from one phase of life to another. The transition or journey may not always be easy, but there is a 'light at the end of the tunnel' to motivate the dreamer.

turkey *see* BIRDS.

turning *see* ACTIONS.

turnips a field of riches. To the lover, a faithful sweetheart (gypsy folklore).

turtle *see tortoise*, ANIMALS.

turtle dove *see* BIRDS.

twelve, twenty-four, two *see* NUMBERS.

typical dreams some dreams are universal. They are common to all races and conditions of people and are accepted by physiologists, psychologists, seers and scientists, to be alike in their frequency of recurrence and of having a certain similarity of content.

The number of typical dreams is necessarily limited; the following list comprises the most universally recognised: FLYING, FALLING, SWIMMING or floating, levitation, NAKEDNESS, standing upon the edge of a precipice, dreams of dead persons, of the death of relatives, losing a tooth or having one drawn, return to schooldays, dreaming of lakes, rivers, etc, dreams of burglars, dreams of climbing.

To the dreams given above Freud adds dreams of missing a train and of the anxiety attendant upon school examinations. He distinguishes four typical erotic dreams: passing through narrow alleys; passing through suites of rooms; being pursued by wild animals, horses, bulls, etc; and being threatened with knives, daggers, etc.

The interpretations of these dreams and their attributed origins are given below.

flying Havelock Ellis (*see* Appendix) termed this as the most usual of the typical dreams. He traces to it the day of man's first transcendent, heavenward thought. It derives its symbolism from the legend of Icarus; the story of the winged feet of Mercury, the tutelary god of the dream. St Jerome and the happy pagan bishop Synesius attributed it to God's grace. According to Ellis, the origin of this dream is physical; it is due to the rhythmic rising and falling of the sleeper's respiratory organs—with the possibility of a snore! In substantiation of this view he instances cases of persons who have drawn near the brink of death, and having lost consciousness, have had the sensation of flying, as though the soul were taking flight.

Freud attributes this dream to erotic sources, with the possibility of several different interpretations.

The flying dream may have its origin in a childhood desire to be freed from conventionality and restraint. He says that this dream is invariably characterized by a keen sense of delight and freedom.

Christians and theosophists construe this dream as a corroboration of their belief in the flight of the spirit.

The gypsy interpretation of flying is as a fortunate dream.

Raphael, on the contrary, qualifies it thus: 'To dream of flying denotes that you will escape many difficulties and dangers. If you dream that you are trying to fly very high you will aspire to a position that you will never reach and for which you are not qualified.'

To servants it means liberty, to the poor it is a dream of riches. To fly very high from the earth without wings signifies fear and danger, as also to fly over the houses and through the streets and forlorn ways signifies trouble and sedition.

hovering, gliding, ascending or rising and falling are attributed generally to the same sources as the dream of flying.

Ellis, however, adds that as a rule the falling dream comes at the end of a flying dream and that being usually accompanied by fear, it presupposes an organic origin, for example a circulatory or nervous trouble, even apoplexy or epilepsy.

Another physical reason for this dream could be that on falling asleep the dreamer does not feel that he is supported by the bed, and that therefore he has the sensation of being in the air, i.e., unsupported.

Freud attributes it to eroticism, as in the case of the flying dream, but adds that in woman it frequently has its origin in the fear of a moral downfall. He classifies it as a typical, sexual dream of fear.

Raphael interprets this dream as foretelling the loss of a sweetheart; to a sailor it augurs shipwreck.

Gypsy folklore tells that it symbolizes losses and crosses, unless the dreamer should pick himself up afterwards, in which case this dream foretells changes and movings.

swimming dreams of swimming are generally attributed to the respiration, but Ellis qualifies this by adding that they are sometimes due to certain sensations on the skin.

Freud holds it to be an erotic dream associated with childhood memories. Raphael's supernatural interpretation of swimming with the head up is a prediction of success in business and in love affairs. Swimming with the head under water in this dream implies trouble and unpleasant news. If you are swimming in dirty water it predicts slander and malice, and if you dream of sinking ruin will follow.

nakedness and being insufficiently clad Freud and Ellis agree that this dream is usually caused by the perception felt in sleep when one has thrown off the covers and is exposed. Freud divides this dream into two varieties, one in which the dreamer is indifferent to his or her condition and perhaps is a reflection of the desire to abandon restraint, and the other in which the dreamer is overwhelmed with shame perhaps reflecting sexual guilt.

The supernatural interpretation is a prediction of a disgrace or embarrassment. To the gypsy interpreters it predicts sickness poverty and general misfortune.

dream of the death of parents or of dead persons Freud takes a rather extreme view and classifies this as a wish dream. He subdivides it under two headings, the dream in which the dreamer is unmoved and the dream in which he or she is grieved. The dream without attendant grief is not a typical dream, in that it is used to symbolize another wish, i.e. it is not the direct desire that someone should die but is a deeper reference to something that the dreamer wants to end. The dream attended by expressions of grief, however deep, is an expression of a desire they feel or have felt at some time in the past, that they want to get rid of the person who died in the dream. Freud gives an example of a woman who dreamed that her siblings suddenly grew wings and flew up into the sky. Of course, he says, the lady wished all her relatives dead or she would not have had this dream.

Other interpretations might take the less controversial view of this dream and translate it as reflecting the dreamer's feelings of sorrow and trouble.

falling out of teeth this dream can be attributed to dental irritation or to people who grind their teeth in their sleep. The Freudian school would define it as an erotic dream, a dream reflecting feelings of sexual insecurity or immaturity.

Oneirocritics agree that it forecasts heavy sorrows. Raphael expresses the general view that to dream that your teeth are very loose predicts personal illness. If one or all come out it denotes an imminent death.

return to school days it is generally thought to be caused by a cramped position of the body or the limbs, suggesting the restraint of a school desk. This dream is often an indication that the dreamer lacks confidence at work or in a relationship.

the examination dream there is the theory that this dream occurs only to persons who have passed an examination, never to those who have failed, but frankly this is doubtful. The recollection of the feeling of not being properly prepared for something, whether it is an exam or not, is common to everyone. The exam dream reflects the feeling of being put under pressure either at work or in a relationship and is not restricted to students.

the dream of missing a train Freud classifies this as a 'consolation dream' directed against a fear, or the fear of dying. The sexual symbolism of the train may also give the interpretation that the dreamer feels sexually inadequate in some way, or unable to cope with a certain relationship. Ellis, on the other hand, attributes dreams of trains and railroads to the physical cause of having a headache.

This dream may indicate physical or mental exhaustion in the dreamer, resentment of missed opportunities or indicate an inability to cope with his or her present life

With a few exceptions the mystical interpreters agree that to see oneself in a railroad train indicates either a change of residence or a long journey. A few hold this dream to mean the visit of a friend from a distance.

climbing a hill, sweating, drawing heavy loads, etc, these dreams might have the physical cause of pulmonary, respiratory or cardiac troubles, manifesting themselves in sleep through the subconscious before the waking mind has recognized them.

The dream of climbing indicates ambition. The analysis depends on how the dreamer progresses. If progress is difficult then there is some obstacle in the way of that ambition.

burglars breaking into the house is attributed to sounds in the environment which become exaggerated by the dream consciousness. Freud, however, traces this dream to erotic sources. The fear of loss or a reflection of feelings of invaded privacy.

Raphael declares that to dream of burglars and to overcome them signifies victory over enemies. To be defeated by the burglars signifies proportionate misfortune.

standing upon the brink of a precipice might be caused by lying diagonally across the bed with the feet extended beyond the edge. It is a dream reflecting an unconscious fear.

Artemidorus and Raphael construe this as a dream of warning. This symbolism can be applied to a psychoanalytic approach too. The dreamer may have an extremely difficult task ahead of him or her causing significant worry, or the precipice may symbolize a choice that has to be made.

lakes, springs, etc Freud suspects dreams of lakes to be of erotic origin, while Raphael says that to dream of a glassy lake denotes prosperity and future happiness. A muddy lake, on the contrary, is supposed to represent loss and heavy cares.

murder the dream of committing murder, while not precisely typical in that it lacks unanimity as to its fundamental source, is nevertheless sufficiently universal to merit mention among the typical dreams.

Freud attributes the dream of murder to the suppressed wish

of the dreamer. Other writers claim that the dream is due to the innate wickedness of the human heart when freed from conventional restraint. Dreaming of committing a murder could be an expression of anger, and of being the victim of a murder reflects feelings of insecurity and victimization.

U

ulcer it was thought that to dream of having an ulcer denoted good health into old age (gypsy folklore). The symbolism is attributable to the idea that ulcers, boils, etc, clear the system. *See also* ABSCESS.

umbrella a dream denoting a sheltered and peaceful life (gypsy folklore). An Eastern symbol of distinction.

uncle or **aunt** a dream denoting family quarrels (gypsy folklore). The symbolism is evidently attributable to the proverbial wicked uncle and guardian.

underground dreams of being underground may indicate a deep exploration of ourselves, or may point to a need to look more closely at the inner self.

Something buried underground may represent a secret, or an aspect of the self that is either repressed or hidden from the rest of the world.

undertaker as a dream of CONTRARY MEANING this forecasts a wedding (gypsy folklore).

underwear *see* CLOTHES.

undressing a dream of undressing suggests the revelation of something that has been kept hidden, or a 'baring of the soul'. Thus it may suggest the giving of oneself in a certain sense, either sexual or spiritual. Undressing may express a desire to be free of constrictions in one's life. *See also* TYPICAL DREAMS.

unguent to use, a dream of profit (gypsy folklore).

unicorn a dream of righteousness (gypsy folklore). The symbolism derives from the unicorn as an ancient emblem of purity.

uniform a dream of glory, valour and celebrity (gypsy folklore).
universal dreams *see* TYPICAL DREAMS.
uphill *see* JOURNEY.
urn a dream of death (gypsy folklore).
usher *see* BRIDE.

V

vagabond sudden journeys or changes from place to place (gypsy folklore). *See also* TINKER and GYPSY.
vagina *see* BODY.
valet concealed, domestic enemy (gypsy folklore).
valise filled it denotes abundance; empty, misery.
valley to dream of walking in a pleasant valley denotes sickness (Raphael). An interpretation in conformity with the modern theory of physical stimuli, and attributing hills, valleys, mountains, etc, to sensations in various parts of the body. Mountains and valleys might also be interpreted as representing the various curves of the body.
vampire images of vampires appearing in dreams may be provoked by Hallowe'en or scary films but not necessarily so. Dreaming of being attacked by a vampire suggests a feeling of being drained by another's dependency, or being weakened by another person's stronger will. Also a dream warning against thieves and other insidious persons (gypsy folklore).
vanishing something that vanishes in a dream may be something or someone that has gone from dreamer's life, or it may be a lost opportunity. To dream of vanishing oneself may be an exploration of the idea of death, or due to poor self-image.
vase labour is signified by this dream (Raphael).
vegetables to dream of eating them denotes sickness (Raphael). Dreaming of vegetables may also be an indication that you think your life is dull.
veil a dream of modesty (gypsy folklore). The veil is a symbol of

hidden things (Tarot). Even now, in many cultures the veil is still a symbol of the submission of woman to man.

veins a dream of trouble and of sorrows (gypsy folklore).

velvet a dream of velvet signifies honour and riches (Artemidorus).

vermin a dream denoting sickness (gypsy folklore). A typical dream in alcohol addicts. *See also rats,* ANIMALS.

viands to see viands or *delicacies* in a dream denotes idleness. If you eat them this denotes sickness (gypsy folklore).

victory a victory over rivals is a dream of success (Raphael).

village *see* CITY.

villagers a dream denoting carefree gaiety (gypsy folklore).

vinegar to dream of drinking vinegar signifies sickness (Artemidorus). This dream may be due to sensory stimuli, acidity, etc.

vines *see* FRUIT.

violence to dream of violence from one from whom you had a right to expect kindness denotes success, promotion because this is a dream of CONTRARY MEANING (Raphael).

violets a ream of violets in season is a dream of success. Out of season they signify lawsuits. Double violets are a symbol of extreme happiness or of pain (gypsy folklore).

violin a dream of social pleasures (gypsy folklore).

viper *see* ANIMALS.

vision to see a vision of a person in a vision or dream is said to denote the death of that person. If the vision is of a place, this denotes disappointment and illusion (gypsy folklore).

voices a dream of merry voices connotes distress and weeping. A dream of wailing voices is one of CONTRARY MEANING signifying joy and merriment (gypsy folklore).

volcano the dream of a volcano denotes family quarrels, disturbances and fights (gypsy folklore).

vow if a vow is broken, the dream denotes misfortune. If the vow is fulfilled this signifies success (gypsy folklore).

voyage *see* JOURNEY.

vulture *see* BIRDS.

W

wading for a girl to dream of wading in clear water denotes a speedy marriage. If she is bathing in muddy water then she is to become involved in an illicit encounter (Raphael).

wake to dream of attending a wake denotes scandalous assertions (gypsy folklore).

walking dreaming of walking in the dirt symbolizes sickness. Walking in the night denotes trouble (gypsy folklore). Walking through WATER is said to symbolize grief. The difficulty experienced by the dreamer in walking through water is a subconscious expression of a difficulty in life. It may be that they are unable to fulfil an aspiration or ambition, or it may be an expression of a difficulty in communicating with someone.

wall just as walls are built in real life to offer protection from the elements or from other people, so the wall in a dream can be read as a defensive image. It stands for the attitudes and postures we may adopt to protect ourselves and our feelings and the face we present to the world when we are sceptical. A wall that surrounds the dreamer may represent a feeling of being 'well-defended', i.e. a feeling of security.

To dream of a wall as an impassable barrier denotes difficulties in the family. Narrow walls are an indication of danger; to ascend without injury denotes success (Raphael). *See also* HOUSE.

walnuts to see or eat them, a sign of trouble and difficulty (Artemidorus).

walrus *see* ANIMALS.

waltz a dream denoting wasted time (gypsy folklore).

war a dream warning of danger of persecution (gypsy folklore).

warbling of BIRDS, assured success (gypsy folklore).

wardrobe *see* FURNITURE.

warehouse dreaming of a warehouse denotes success and accumulation of possessions through frugality and saving (gypsy folklore).

washing *see* WATER.

wasps *see* INSECTS and STING.

watch a good dream denoting success (gypsy folklore).

watchman loss through theft, a dream of warning (gypsy folklore).

water water is essential to life and, therefore, inevitably has a certain importance in dreams.

Dreaming of the SEA may indicate an awareness of the depth of our unconsciousness, the subconscious knowledge that our inner selves go much deeper than our immediate awareness.

The vastness of the sea or the OCEAN reflects the huge realm of the unconscious. Surging waves in a dream may indicate a feeling in the dreamer of the life energies that flow within, the unknown forces between will and action, for example.

Waves, and the ebb and flow of the tide, may represent the ebb and flow of human emotions, from negative to positive and back again.

Images of SWIMMING in a deep pool may represent a regressive wish on the part of the dreamer with the pool symbolizing the amniotic fluid within the womb. Consequently, to dream of coming out of a pool of water may be indicative of a new start in life, or a wish for such a thing.

To dream of DROWNING, if FEAR is present, may indicate a fear of death; to dream of simply sinking underwater, without any feelings of an unpleasant nature, may indicate either a wish to explore one's unconscious in more depth, or an exploration of the idea of death.

Images of *washing* in a dream may indicate a desire for moral or spiritual cleansing, or a feeling that one has been cleansed of a particular feeling or emotion. To dream of washing oneself denotes good health after an illness or a change for the better (gypsy folklore). *See also* FOUNTAIN; WALKING.

water-bearer always a good dream (gypsy folklore).

water mill a favourable dream (gypsy folklore).

watermelon *see* FRUIT.

waves *see* WATER.

wax a dream denoting an unstable character, doubt on the part of the dreamer (gypsy folklore). *See also* BEES.

wax candle *see* CANDLE.

wealth a dream of CONTRARY MEANING forecasting sickness, even death (gypsy folklore).

weapons weapons are generally symbols of aggression, either sexual, emotional or physical. The situation and the type of weapon may give a clue as to the nature of the aggression (for example, a GUN or a *cannon* may be symbols for the phallus; the discharge of these weapons representing EJACULATION). *See also* KNIFE and AGGRESSION.

weasel *see* ANIMALS.

weather if the weather is good this is a dream denoting deceptive security. *See also* STORM.

weathercock denotes fickle friends (Artemidorus).

weaving a dream of weaving denotes success in trade (Raphael).

wedding dreams of a wedding in which the dreamer is the bride or the groom may be wish-fulfilment. Alternatively, a wedding may indicate a close spiritual or emotional tie, in other words, 'a marriage of two minds'. This may be a dream of CONTRARY MEANING denoting a FUNERAL. If the dreamer is ill, his own death is denoted (gypsy folklore).

wedding ring *see* LOSS.

weeding a dream of health, wealth and happiness (Raphael).

weeds a dream of much labour and small benefit (gypsy folklore).

weeping a dream of CONTRARY MEANING denoting joy (gypsy folklore).

whale *see* ANIMALS.

wharf to dream of a wharf denotes assurance of safety (gypsy folklore).

wheat a dream denoting great wealth (gypsy folklore).

wheel the wheel may be an image of the life cycle, the continuum of birth, life and death. It may also represent one's fortune, like the spin of the roulette wheel. The wheel is a symbol of eternity, and therefore a happy dream (gypsy folklore).

whip to dream of whipping an ANIMAL denotes sorrow to you; to dream of being whipped is said to predict an imminent scandal (gypsy folklore). The whip was a symbol of martyrdom.

whirlpool a dream warning you of danger, physical or otherwise (gypsy folklore). The dreams of whirling or of being whirled are readily attributable to physical causes, headaches, vertigo, etc.

whirlwind heavy troubles (gypsy folklore). For physical causes *see* WHIRLPOOL.

whisper to dream of whispering or hearing a whisper denotes scandal (gypsy folklore).

white *see* COLOURS.

widowhood a dream of CONTRARY MEANING denoting satisfaction and joy (gypsy folklore).

wife to a woman this dream predicts that she will never be a wife; to a man this predicts his wife's illness and recovery (gypsy folklore).

wig a dream warning the dreamer of peril ahead (gypsy folklore). A dream of a wig may reflect a subconscious insecurity about one's appearance, or it may symbolize something that the dreamer wants to hide.

wildcat *see* ANIMALS.

wilderness a warning that the dreamer's friends will prove false and that he must rely on his own judgements (gypsy folklore).

will to dream of making your own will denotes depression. To dream of another making a will denotes a wish to profit from the industry of someone else.

willow a dream of sorrow and grief (gypsy folklore). Old English writers associate this plant with graves and mourning.

wind the wind is thought to represent the motivating forces and external influences that 'blow' us along in life, as distinct from conscious wishes and desires.

A moderate breeze is a dream of joyful tidings. Strong winds predict arguments in love and in all matters (gypsy folklore).

windmill changes for the better (gypsy folklore).

window to sit at one forecasts slanderous reports. To set a light in one symbolizes knowledge (gypsy folklore), deriving from the window being an ancient symbol of knowledge.

wine to dream of drinking, health, wealth, etc (gypsy folklore). To dream of drinking in moderation might well imply strength and refreshment through sensory stimuli. Some dream interpreters translate this as a forecast of the dreamer's marriage.

wings to dream of having wings was thought to forecast your own death, or that of the person to whom they are attached (gypsy folklore). Wings were the symbol of immortality and evoke images of angels.

Dreaming of having wings could simply be the expression of a wish to be more independent, or of escaping an unpleasant situation.

wire a dream denoting loss of liberty. Gold wire denotes utter poverty, while iron wire was thought to symbolize drunkenness (gypsy folklore).

witchcraft misfortune to the dreamer and his family (gypsy folklore). This interpretation may have been made for the possible purpose of inspiring an awe of the black art.

wolf *see lion*, ANIMALS.

womb dreams of returning to the womb or dreams that contain symbols that may represent such a desire suggest either the dreamer's desire to be free of a sense of responsibility, to cease to be answerable for his or her actions, or the dreamer's desire for a sense of security that he or she feels is lacking in waking life.

wood *see* JOURNEY.

wool to buy or to sell wool is a dream of prosperity and abundance (gypsy folklore).

work to be tired from work is a dream of sickness. To see men at work denotes success in business. To work with the right hand signifies good fortune and with the left embarrassment (gypsy folklore).

workhouse to dream of being in one denotes a legacy (gypsy folklore).

workshop a dream of thrift and wealth (gypsy folklore).

worms *see* ANIMALS.

wormwood a dream predicting bitter trials (gypsy folklore). Because of its taste and medicinal effect wormwood was an ancient symbol of bitterness.

wound a person who dreams of being wounded may have had some experience in the past from which he or she has not yet recovered mentally. A man who dreams of severe injury may have a fear of CASTRATION. Women may dream of MENSTRUATION as a wound, or the wound may represent loss of virginity (about which she possibly has negative feelings). Wounds may also represent emotional distress.

wrapping paper *see* PAPER.

wreath a dream of triumph (gypsy folklore). The symbolism derives from the wreath being a pagan emblem of triumph.

wreck a dream of a wreck denotes misfortunes to come (gypsy folklore).

wrinkles to dream of seeing wrinkles in your own face promises that you will live to a great age (Raphael).

wrist *see* BODY.

writing writing is mostly a symbol for communication. A promise of surprise through a letter (gypsy folklore). *See also* TALKING.

writing paper *see* PAPER.

Y

yacht to see a yacht in clear, smooth water denotes success. If the yacht is at sail in stormy seas, the reverse is signified.

yarn a dream denoting inheritance and powerful friends (gypsy folklore).

yawning if you dream that you are yawning it is a warning to beware of surprises (gypsy folklore).

yeast a dream symbolizing the stirring of discontent (gypsy folklore).

yew tree a dream of this tree denotes honour and great wealth (gypsy folklore). The yew was a sacred tree amongst the Romans and the early Britons, who prized it especially in the manufacture of bows.

yoke to dream of wearing a yoke denotes anger (gypsy folklore).

young to dream of becoming youthful denotes a faithful and loving partner or spouse.

Z

zebra *see* ANIMALS.

zephyr inconstancy is predicted by this dream (gypsy folklore). A symbol of lightness and fickleness.

zero a dream denoting a rise to the apex of power and fortune (gypsy folklore). *See also* NUMBERS.

zinc a dream connoting the distrust of friends (gypsy folklore).

zither a message from a lover is augured by this dream.

zodiac to dream of the twelve signs of the zodiac shows a great traveller, and predicts a voyage around the world (gypsy folklore).

zoo dreams of a zoo in which all the ANIMALS are contented and in which the mood is obviously optimistic, may indicate a desire, that the dreamer may not have expressed in waking life, to exist within the confines of a family unit or similar setup.

Dreams of a more unpleasant nature, where the animals are distressed, would indicate unhappiness in the dreamer and a deep sense of frustration with his or her present situation in waking life.

Interpretation of Dreams by the Ancient Art of Geomancy

"These whimsical pictures, inasmuch as they originate from us, may well have an analogy with our whole life and fate"— Goethe.

In 1830 Raphael, the "astrologer of the Nineteenth Century," published a "Royal Book of Dreams," which he claimed to have unearthed in the form of an ancient manuscript and in which he gives a full explanation of Geomancy, the art of dream interpretation. Another early authority was M. Nicolas Oudot in 1669, who published explaining the translation of dreams by means of the ancient art of Geomancy.

The art of Geomancy, or divining by the earth, received its name from ancient diviners who drew their magic figures upon earth before inks and pens had come into general use. Two Greek words—Ge, the earth, and Manteai, prophecy— go to make up the term. The art is respectfully referred to by Chaucer, Dryden and others, while in later times Sir Edward Bulwer-Lytton is supposed to have made frequent experiments with it. In more recent times it has been chiefly practised by the Chinese, in the Sudan, Egypt, and in India, in which countries its votaries were frequently to be seen drawing geomantic figures upon the sand or in the dusts of the street. A small stick and earth, dust or well cleaned sand were employed by the Chaldeans, Egyptians, Persians and Hebrews, when papyrus and parchment were only for the elect.

The theory of Geomancy in dream interpretation is the application of subconsciousness to the mechanical production of certain groups of ciphers, lines, dots or asterisks. Each group when divided according to directions forms a figure which bears a specific meaning. The accuracy of this method of tapping the subconscious cannot, in our present state of knowledge, be vouched for as infallible or as wholly unreliable. While many scoff at the system, it nevertheless has its followers who contend that curious and satisfactory results have attended this process of dream interpretation.

Directions for use of Geomancy are simple. With a pencil mark down ten lines of stars. Do not count the number of stars placed in the lines, as this should be left to chance, or the subconscious. While marking down the lines of stars the inquirer should think intently of the dream that he or she wishes to interpret, silently demanding to know its true meaning.

Illustration of the Process

Line

1 ★ ★ ★ ★ ★ ★ ★ ★ ★ ★ ★ ★
2 ★ ★ ★ ★ ★ ★ ★ ★
3 ★ ★ ★ ★ ★ ★ ★ ★ ★ ★
4 ★ ★ ★ ★ ★
5 ★ ★ ★
6 ★ ★ ★ ★
7 ★ ★ ★ ★ ★ ★
8 ★ ★ ★
9 ★ ★ ★ ★ ★
10 ★ ★ ★ ★ ★ ★ ★ ★ ★ ★

These stars, however roughly drawn, should be made at random, the inquirer merely keeping count of the number of columns, which are invariably ten in number as above.

They should then be grouped after the following system:

In the first line there are twelve asterisks, an even number, hence in the figure are written two asterisks:　★ ★ 1

In the second line there are eight asterisks, also an even number:　★ ★ 2

In the third line there are eleven, an odd number, hence
write one asterisk: ★ 3
In the fourth line there are five (odd)   ★ 4
In the fifth line there are three (odd)   ★ 5

The second figure falls as follows
Sixth line, four asterisks (even)   ★ ★ 6
Seventh line, six (even)   ★ ★ 7
Eight line, three asterisks (odd)   ★ 8
Ninth line, five (odd)   ★ 9
Tenth line, eleven asterisks (odd)   ★ 10

The two signs are placed side by side and a third figure
called the index figure made from combining them thus.

First Figure   Second Figure   Third or Index Figure
   ★   ★   ★   ★   ★   ★
   ★   ★   ★   ★   ★   ★
      ★   ★   ★   ★
      ★   ★   ★   ★
      ★   ★   ★   ★

Referring to the Index of Hieroglyphical Emblems given
below we find that the figure formed by combining figures
one and two is found under the sign Aries. Turning from the
index table to the page devoted to translating figures that
come under the hieroglyphic Aries we find the interpretation
to be as follows. "This dream indicates a great change in the
fortune of the dreamer; wealth and friends await you."

Raphael, the great authority on dreams, speaks of this
method of interpretation: "The occult principle of the soul
shall so guide and counsel the dreamer (or diviner) and
control his hand so that he shall mark down those signatures
which will convey a true answer."

Index of Hieroglyphic Emblems

Aries	Sol	Taurus	Jove	Gemini	Luna	Cancer	Saturn
★ ★	★ ★	★	★	★ ★	★ ★	★ ★	★ ★
★ ★	★ ★	★	★	★ ★	★	★ ★	★ ★
★ ★	★	★	★	★	★ ★	★ ★	★ ★
★ ★	★	★	★ ★	★	★ ★	★	★ ★
★ ★	★	★	★ ★	★	★ ★	★ ★	★

Leo	Mars	Virgo	Mercury	Libra	Venus	Scorpio	Pallas
★	★	★ ★	★	★	★	★ ★	★ ★
★ ★	★ ★	★	★ ★	★	★	★	★ ★
★ ★	★ ★	★	★	★	★	★	★ ★
★ ★	★ ★	★	★	★ ★	★	★	★
★ ★	★	★ ★	★	★	★ ★	★	★

Sagit.	Juno	Capricorn	Ceres	Aquarius	Vesta	Pisces	Diana
★	★	★	★ ★	★	★ ★	★	★ ★
★	★	★ ★	★	★ ★	★	★ ★	★ ★
★ ★	★ ★	★ ★	★ ★	★	★ ★	★	★
★ ★	★ ★	★	★	★ ★	★	★ ★	★ ★
★ ★	★	★	★	★	★ ★	★ ★	★

Medusa	Phoebus	Hecate	Apollo	Fortuna	Neptune	Orion	Finis
★ ★	★	★	★ ★	★ ★	★ ★	★	★
★	★ ★	★ ★	★	★ ★	★	★	★
★ ★	★ ★	★	★	★	★	★ ★	★ ★
★ ★	★	★	★ ★	★	★ ★	★	★
★	★ ★	★ ★	★	★ ★	★ ★	★ ★	★

First Roll of Oracles

Hieroglyphic Emblem

★	★
★	★
★	★
★	★
★	★

	Sign			
1		**2**		**ARIES**

★	★	★	★	This dream indicates great changes
★	★	★	★	in the fortune of the dreamer; wealth
	★		★	and friends await you.
	★		★	
	★		★	

★	★	★	★	A merry dream of celebrations and
	★		★	feasting.
	★		★	
	★		★	
	★		★	

★	★	★	★	A dream of disappointments.
★	★	★	★	
★	★	★	★	
	★		★	
	★		★	

★	★	★	★	Your dream warns of a taciturn
★	★	★	★	enemy.
★	★	★	★	
★	★	★	★	
	★		★	

★	★	★	★	A dream of voyages, waters and
★	★	★	★	flitting from place to place.
★	★	★	★	
★	★	★	★	
★	★	★	★	

	★		★	This vision has little or no
	★		★	significance.
	★		★	
	★		★	
	★		★	

143

★ ★   ★ ★   A sign of anger, high words and
  ★   ★   contention. Be careful to eschew
★ ★   ★ ★   strife.
★ ★   ★ ★
★ ★   ★ ★

★ ★   ★ ★   This dream is connected with a
★ ★   ★ ★   multitude of business and great
  ★   ★   deeds.
  ★   ★
  ★   ★

★ ★   ★ ★   A dream of warning: you will be
★ ★   ★ ★   tempted to travel but accidents and
★ ★   ★ ★   danger threaten. Do not travel.
  ★   ★
★ ★   ★ ★

  ★   ★   A joyous dream foretelling happiness
★ ★   ★ ★   and feasting.
★ ★   ★ ★
★ ★   ★ ★
★ ★   ★ ★

★ ★   ★ ★   News of distant friends or relatives is
  ★   ★   here predicted.
  ★   ★
  ★   ★
★ ★   ★ ★

  ★   ★   This dream indicates funerals,
★ ★   ★ ★   burials, grief.
★ ★   ★ ★
★ ★   ★ ★
  ★   ★

  ★   ★   A dream of warning; beware of a
  ★   ★   secret enemy.
  ★   ★
  ★   ★
★ ★   ★ ★

  ★   ★   Avoid travel and dangers; beware of
  ★   ★   an alarm or fright.
  ★   ★
★ ★   ★ ★
  ★   ★

To a man this dream forecasts joy, the company of women, marriage.

This dream is of little importance to a male; to a female it foretells society, happiness and the attainment of desire.

Sad and ominous, forecasting bereavements, griefs and tears.

A dream of misfortune. Prepare yourself by avoiding speculation and risks.

Cheerful happy fortune; the accomplishment of desires.

Good fortune; in business profit far beyond your expectation.

Crosses to lovers; disappointments to tradesmen.

Crosses, thwarted purposes, failures.

★ ★ ★ ★	For several months after this dream you will have journeys and various unsettled conditions.
★ ★ ★ ★	Curiously ominous; cares, toils, harassments. Proceed cautiously.
★ ★ ★ ★	Thieves, losses or fire threatened. Beware of losing goods and money.
★ ★ ★ ★	Disappointment, deception, vain hopes.
★ ★ ★ ★	Prosperity and increase of business.
★ ★ ★ ★	A sad dream; you will have a funeral in your family or perhaps lose a loved friend.
★ ★ ★ ★	Bereavement, the loss of a valuable friend.
★ ★ ★ ★	The friendship of powerful people.

★　　　★　　　　　　Shifting fortunes, sudden gains,
★　★　★　★　　　losses, triumphs, perplexities.
　★　　　★
　★　　　★
★　★　★　★

★　★　★　★　　　Conquests, triumph over enemies and
★　★　★　★　　　antagonists.
　★　　　★
　★　　　★
★　★　★　★

Hieroglyphic Emblem　★　★
　　　　　　　　　　　★　★
　　　　　　　　　　　　★
　　　　　　　　　　　　★
　　　　　　　　　　　　★

| | Sign | |
| 1 | | 2 |

SOL

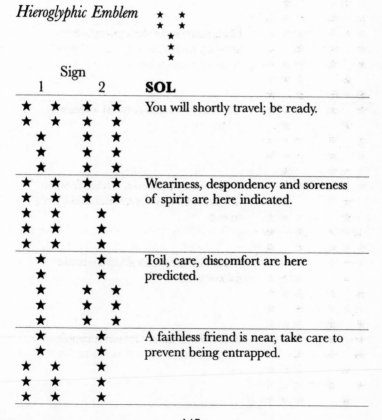

★　★　★　★　　　You will shortly travel; be ready.
★　★　★　★
　★　　★　★
　★　　★　★
　★　　★　★

★　★　★　★　　　Weariness, despondency and soreness
★　★　★　★　　　of spirit are here indicated.
★　★　★
★　★　★
★　★　★

　★　　　★　　　Toil, care, discomfort are here
　★　　　★　　　predicted.
　★　　★　★
　★　　★　★
　★　　★　★

　★　　　★　　　A faithless friend is near, take care to
　★　　　★　　　prevent being entrapped.
★　★　★
★　★　★
★　★　★

147

★   ★
★   ★
★   ★ ★
★ ★ ★
★ ★ ★

Fighting and possible bloodshed, also legal entanglements. Avoid giving offence.

★   ★
★   ★
★ ★ ★
  ★ ★ ★
  ★ ★ ★

A dream of quarrelling and falsehood.

★ ★ ★ ★
★ ★ ★ ★
  ★ ★ ★
★ ★ ★
★ ★ ★

Illness is predicted. Avoid excitement.

★ ★ ★ ★
★ ★ ★ ★
★ ★ ★
  ★ ★ ★
  ★ ★ ★

Friends are indicated, except on the first day of the moon, when this dream augurs a legacy.

★ ★ ★ ★
  ★ ★
★ ★ ★
★ ★ ★
★ ★ ★

You will receive a gift, but beware of treachery.

★ ★ ★ ★
  ★ ★
  ★ ★ ★
  ★ ★ ★
  ★ ★ ★

Unimportant, save on Saturday when this dream forecasts trouble and sorrow.

★ ★ ★ ★
★ ★ ★ ★
★ ★ ★
  ★ ★ ★
★ ★ ★

After this dream avoid speculation and betting.

★ ★ ★ ★
★ ★ ★ ★
  ★ ★ ★
★ ★ ★
  ★ ★ ★

Better fortunes are in store for the dreamer whose troubles are nearly over.

★ ★	★ ★	Heavy clouds and annoyances surround the dreamer.

★ ★	★ ★	News, also the illness or death of a near relative or kind friend.

★ ★	★ ★	The stars will be with you for three years; you shall prosper.

★ ★	★ ★	A happy dream; legacies before three years.

★	★	Joy, mirth and a wedding are at hand.

★	★	To a female a betrothal, to a male the love of a fair woman.

★	★	Beware a thief who lives nearby.

★	★	An evil dream denoting joy ending in sorrow.

★ ★ ★ ★ 　★ 　 ★ 　★ ★ ★ 　★ ★ ★ ★ ★ ★	The imprisonment of a friend will greatly trouble you.
★ ★ ★ ★ 　★ 　 ★ ★ ★ 　 ★ ★ ★ 　 ★ 　★ ★ ★	Do not leave your home the day after this dream in case you meet with sorrow and harm.
★ 　 ★ 　★ 　 ★ 　★ ★ ★ ★ ★ 　 ★ 　★ ★ ★	Disappointed hopes, anger, quarrelling and contention are indicated.
★ 　 ★ 　★ 　 ★ ★ ★ 　 ★ 　★ ★ ★ ★ ★ 　 ★	An absent friend will visit you.
★ 　 ★ 　★ 　 ★ 　★ ★ ★ 　★ ★ ★ ★ ★ 　 ★	Slander is aimed at you.
★ 　 ★ 　★ 　 ★ ★ ★ 　 ★ ★ ★ 　 ★ 　★ ★ ★	Temporary misfortune and trouble are predicted.
★ 　 ★ ★ ★ ★ ★ ★ ★ 　 ★ 　★ ★ ★ 　★ ★ ★	Evil and disappointment are here denoted, save on the second and third days of the moon.
★ 　 ★ ★ ★ ★ ★ 　★ ★ ★ ★ ★ 　 ★ ★ ★ 　 ★	Important matters concerning your welfare, also a journey within a short time.

★ ★ ★ ★				Wealth in plenty, a dream implying fortunate stars of destiny.

★ ★ ★ ★
  ★   ★
★ ★ ★
  ★   ★ ★
  ★   ★ ★

Wealth in plenty, a dream implying fortunate stars of destiny.

★ ★ ★ ★
  ★   ★
  ★   ★ ★
★ ★ ★
★ ★ ★

An auspicious dream. You are destined to fortune and many friends.

  ★   ★
★ ★ ★ ★
  ★   ★ ★
★ ★ ★
  ★   ★ ★

To mariners a rough voyage, to others stormy times ahead.

  ★   ★
★ ★ ★ ★
★ ★ ★
  ★   ★ ★
★ ★ ★

You will find treasure, or will recover something that has been lost.

Hieroglyphic Emblem
★
★
★
★
★

	Sign		**TAURUS**
1		2	

  ★   ★ ★
  ★   ★ ★
  ★   ★ ★
  ★   ★ ★
  ★   ★ ★

An obscure and unimportant dream.

★ ★ ★
★ ★ ★
★ ★ ★
★ ★ ★
★ ★ ★

Trouble, severe but transient, is at hand.

A fortunate dream save on a Saturday when it forecasts ill.

The dreamer will shortly receive money.

This dream bodes heavy expenses, the losing and paying away of money.

Financial difficulties, loss and vexation in business.

New friends who will benefit the dreamer.

A malicious enemy is watching the dreamer, let him beware.

The dreamer is warned against deceit, enemies and treachery, also mental depression.

	★		★	★	Sorrow and blighted hopes.
★		★		★	
	★		★	★	
	★		★	★	
	★		★	★	

★		★		★	Unpleasant suggestions through
★		★		★	letters and papers.
★		★			
	★		★	★	
	★		★		

	★		★	★	The dreamer will triumph over rivals
	★		★	★	in business and love.
	★		★	★	
★		★	★		
	★		★		

★		★		★	An unlucky dream: avoid irritating
★		★		★	your enemies.
★		★		★	
★		★		★	
	★		★	★	

	★		★	★	Avoid a tall, dark, taciturn person; he
	★		★	★	seeks to harm you.
	★		★	★	
	★		★	★	
★		★			

	★		★	★	A fortunate dream, forecasting good
★		★	★		news and gratified wishes.
★		★	★		
★		★	★		
★		★	★		

★		★	★		A pleasant dream denoting merry-
	★		★	★	making, joy, prosperity. The object of
	★		★	★	the dreamer's affection is sincere.
	★		★	★	
	★		★	★	

Prepare for travelling; you shall take a fortunate journey.

Journeys, changes, agitation, the arrival of friends long absent.

Depression, the weight of cares and troubles.

Loss through carelessness and neglect; a warning to take care.

A dream warning the dreamer to be careful of his signature and of signing papers.

A dream of disappointment in love and in business.

A favourable dream for both love and finance.

A troubled dream to lovers; to others diverse fortunes through strange planetary influences.

154

Letters containing evil news will upset you.

Slander and false rumours will attack your credit.

Deceitful friends whom you trusted will prove your greatest enemies.

Sickness will afflict those whom you love most.

Annoyance concerning papers or documents which will not arrive in time.

Letters and news from those who have long been silent are approaching.

A fortunate dream forecasting prosperity and changes for the better.

Losses are predicted; to the lover parting with his beloved.

Hieroglyphic Emblem

```
            ★
            ★
            ★
          ★   ★
          ★   ★
```

	Sign		
	1		2

JOVE

Sign 1	Sign 2	
★ ★ ★	A change is near at hand.
★ ★ ★	
★ ★ ★	
★ ★ ★ ★	
★ ★ ★ ★	

```
★   ★       ★
★   ★       ★
★   ★       ★
★   ★   ★   ★
★   ★   ★   ★
```
Prepare for a journey across the water.

```
    ★       ★   ★
    ★       ★   ★
    ★       ★   ★
    ★       ★
    ★       ★
```
On the third day of the month this dream predicts loss; ordinarily, however, it is unimportant.

```
★   ★       ★
★   ★       ★
★   ★       ★
    ★       ★
    ★       ★
```
An unfortunate dream; guard your home.

```
★   ★       ★
★   ★       ★
    ★   ★   ★
★   ★   ★   ★
★   ★   ★   ★
```
This dream indicates that your letters are intercepted. Take care.

```
    ★       ★   ★
    ★       ★   ★
★   ★       ★
★   ★   ★   ★
★   ★   ★   ★
```
Family cares and sorrows are here foretold.

```
★   ★       ★
    ★       ★   ★
★   ★       ★
★   ★       ★
★   ★   ★   ★
```
Your homeland is subject to perils.

★ ★ ★ ★ ★ ★ ★ ★ ★ ★ ★ ★ ★ ★ ★ ★ ★	You are threatened with a fright or alarm.
★ ★ ★ ★ ★ ★ ★ ★ ★ ★ ★ ★ ★ ★ ★	Before long you will lose a near relative.
★ ★ ★ ★ ★ ★ ★ ★ ★ ★ ★ ★ ★ ★ ★	Scandals and many cares here are prophesied.
★ ★ ★ ★ ★ ★ ★ ★ ★ ★ ★ ★ ★ ★ ★	An old, half-forgotten grievance will be vigorously revived.
★ ★ ★ ★ ★ ★ ★ ★ ★ ★ ★ ★ ★ ★ ★	This vision is an omen of anger and angry words.
★ ★ ★ ★ ★ ★ ★ ★ ★ ★ ★ ★ ★ ★ ★ ★ ★	A more propitious fortune is here augured, one over which the dreamer may well rejoice.
★ ★ ★ ★ ★ ★ ★ ★ ★ ★ ★ ★ ★ ★ ★ ★ ★	Extraordinary news from friends; much action for the next three months.
★ ★ ★ ★ ★ ★ ★ ★ ★ ★ ★ ★ ★ ★ ★ ★	An ill-omened dream.

Peril, grief and secret sorrows at home are foretold.

Beware of horses and of riding.

An ominous dream of old grievances renewed.

Rejoicings and merry-making; weddings.

Joy and mirth are here foretold.

The dreamer will shortly receive a charming invitation.

Grief and misfortune attend this dream.

The dreamer is subject to evil influences of which he should beware.

★ ★ ★ ★ ★ ★ ★ ★ ★ ★ ★ ★ ★ ★ ★	You will find a new and helpful friend within the month.	

★ ★ ★ ★ ★ ★ ★ ★ ★ ★ ★ ★ ★ ★ ★	Loss, especially if dreamed on the third day of the moon.	

★ ★ ★ ★ ★ ★ ★ ★ ★ ★ ★ ★ ★ ★ ★	This dream forecasts disputes, avoid them.	

★ ★ ★ ★ ★ ★ ★ ★ ★ ★ ★ ★ ★ ★ ★	You shall find three strong friends within the year.	

★ ★ ★ ★ ★ ★ ★ ★ ★ ★ ★ ★ ★ ★ ★	If you are single this dream forecasts marriage.	

★ ★ ★ ★ ★ ★ ★ ★ ★ ★ ★ ★ ★ ★ ★	If your dream was terrifying have no fear, it is not harmful.	

★ ★ ★ ★ ★ ★ ★ ★ ★ ★ ★ ★ ★ ★ ★	Frame your speech with care; quarrelling is shown.	

★ ★ ★ ★ ★ ★ ★ ★ ★ ★ ★ ★ ★	Your dream signifies that the times are opposed to your success.	

★	★	★		Of whatever this vision may consist
★	★	★		have no fear of harm.
	★	★	★	
	★	★		
	★	★		

Hieroglyphic Emblem ★ ★
★ ★
★
★ ★
★ ★

Sign
1   2   **GEMINI**

★	★	★	★	Journeys or crossing deep waters are
★	★	★	★	foreshadowed.
	★	★	★	
★	★	★	★	
★	★	★	★	

★	★	★	★	Increased business affairs are much to
★	★	★	★	do with writing and documents.
★	★	★		
★	★	★	★	
★	★	★	★	

★		★		The death of an enemy to your
★		★		peace of mind is here foretold.
★		★	★	
★		★		
★		★		

★		★		Something that you have long wished
★		★		for has gone by.
★	★	★		
★		★		
★		★		

★	★	★	★	Good fortune and money are here
★	★	★	★	foretold.
	★	★	★	
	★	★		
	★	★		

★	★	★	★	Profit through some business
★	★	★	★	transaction or bargain.
★	★		★	
	★		★	
	★		★	

★			★	Victory over enemies.
★			★	
★		★	★	
★	★	★	★	
★	★	★	★	

★			★	Merry-making and festivities to
★			★	which you shall be invited.
★	★		★	
★	★	★	★	
★	★	★	★	

★	★	★	★	You are warned of deceit among
	★		★	your friends and of sickness in your
★	★		★	home.
★	★	★	★	
★	★	★	★	

★	★	★	★	Trouble from treacherous and
	★		★	scornful enemies, but final victory
	★	★	★	over them.
★	★	★	★	
★	★	★	★	

★	★	★	★	Whatever you have on hand will,
★	★	★	★	on the morning after this dream,
★	★		★	bring you trouble.
	★		★	
★	★	★	★	

★	★	★	★	Expect letters and news from friends
★	★	★	★	long absent.
	★		★	
	★		★	
★	★	★	★	

★	★	★	★	Sadness and sorrow are here predicted.
★	★	★	★	
★	★		★	
★	★	★	★	
	★		★	

★ ★ ★ ★   Death will soon rob you of a near and
★ ★ ★ ★   dear friend.
  ★   ★ ★
★ ★ ★ ★
  ★   ★

  ★   ★   A jovial, happy dream.
★ ★ ★ ★
★ ★   ★
★ ★ ★ ★
★ ★ ★ ★

  ★   ★   A dream of regret for vanished joys.
★ ★ ★ ★
  ★   ★ ★
★ ★ ★ ★
★ ★ ★ ★

  ★   ★   A loss by thieves is here forecast.
★ ★ ★ ★
★ ★   ★
★ ★ ★ ★
  ★   ★

  ★   ★   Beware of treacherous enemies near at
★ ★ ★ ★   hand.
  ★   ★ ★
★ ★ ★ ★
  ★   ★

★ ★ ★ ★   Marriage within the year is here
  ★   ★   predicted.
  ★   ★ ★
  ★   ★
★ ★ ★ ★

★ ★ ★ ★   A dream of great profit unless it is
  ★   ★   dreamed on the first day of a new
★ ★   ★   moon or in an eclipse.
  ★   ★
★ ★ ★ ★

  ★   ★   A dream of friendship to all, but to a
★ ★ ★ ★   male the love of a beautiful woman is
  ★   ★ ★   promised.
  ★   ★
  ★   ★

★   ★
★ ★ ★ ★
★ ★   ★
  ★   ★
  ★   ★
	This dream warns you of trouble.

★ ★ ★ ★ ★ ★ ★ ★ ★ ★ ★ ★ ★	A 'wearyful' dream.
★ ★ ★ ★ ★ ★ ★ ★ ★ ★ ★ ★ ★	Harassment, even possible imprisonment is forecast by this dream.
★ ★ ★ ★ ★ ★ ★ ★ ★ ★ ★ ★ ★	An evil dream; disappointed hopes.
★ ★ ★ ★ ★ ★ ★ ★ ★ ★ ★ ★ ★	Troubles overshadow your home.

★ ★ ★ ★
  ★   ★
  ★ ★ ★
  ★   ★
  ★   ★
	A dream assuring you that the stars are propitious to a return of fortune.

★ ★ ★ ★
  ★   ★
★ ★ ★
  ★   ★
  ★   ★
	On Friday this dream foretells deceit; on Monday a journey; on other days a new friend.

★ ★ ★ ★
  ★   ★
★ ★ ★
★ ★ ★ ★
  ★   ★
	Quarrels and unhappiness are here indicated.

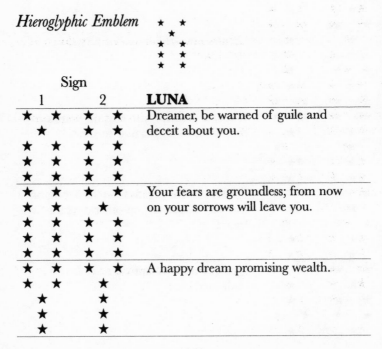

★	★	★	★	This dream proceeds from ill-health.
	★		★	
	★		★	★
★	★		★	★
	★		★	

	★			★	Joy, mirth and pleasure are here
★	★		★	★	denoted.
	★		★	★	
	★		★	
★	★		★	★

	★			★	Unfavourable; danger of discredit or
★	★		★	★	of loss of goods.
★	★		★	
	★		★	
★	★		★	★

Hieroglyphic Emblem

```
★   ★
  ★
★   ★
★   ★
★   ★
```

	Sign	
1		2	**LUNA**

★	★	★	★	Dreamer, be warned of guile and
	★		★	★	deceit about you.
★	★		★	★	
★	★		★	★	
★	★		★	★	

★	★	★	★	Your fears are groundless; from now
★	★		★		on your sorrows will leave you.
★	★		★	★	
★	★		★	★	
★	★		★	★	

★	★	★	★	A happy dream promising wealth.
★	★		★	
	★		★	
	★		★	
	★		★	

Seven years of good fortune are promised by this dream.

Voyages and changes are here denoted.

Voyages and journeys and adventure with a pleasant companion.

Trouble to some of your absent friends is indicated.

Losses in your family circle are foretold by this.

You will be busy over books and papers.

Hasty news is forecast.

A legacy will follow this dream.

```
★  ★  ★  ★
   ★     ★  ★
★  ★  ★  ★
   ★        ★
★  ★  ★  ★
```
Favourable times await the dreamer.

```
★  ★  ★  ★
★  ★     ★
★  ★  ★  ★
★  ★  ★  ★
   ★        ★
```
A dream forecasting death among your relatives and friends.

```
★  ★  ★  ★
   ★     ★  ★
★  ★  ★  ★
★  ★  ★  ★
   ★        ★
```
A dream warning you of sickness.

```
   ★        ★
★  ★     ★
★  ★  ★  ★
★  ★  ★  ★
★  ★  ★  ★
```
A fortunate dream promising you gold and silver.

```
   ★        ★
   ★     ★  ★
★  ★  ★  ★
★  ★  ★  ★
★  ★  ★  ★
```
The dreamer will discover a secret.

```
   ★        ★
★  ★     ★
★  ★  ★  ★
★  ★  ★  ★
   ★        ★
```
A dream of sickness and calamity.

```
   ★        ★
   ★     ★  ★
★  ★  ★  ★
★  ★  ★  ★
   ★        ★
```
A bad dream forecasting trouble, sickness, etc.

```
★  ★  ★  ★
   ★     ★  ★
★  ★  ★  ★
   ★        ★
★  ★  ★  ★
```
Prepare for a change of residence.

Favourable times draw near; expect to receive money.

A removal is hereby indicated.

Confusion and possible loss among papers, deeds and documents.

A difficult month; be warned of losses.

Mischief surrounds the dreamer who is warned to act cautiously.

Be warned of a funeral within the year.

A dream of fickle fortune and of trouble.

Good fortune, money, presents, prosperity are predicted.

★	★	★	★
	★	★	★
★	★	★	★
	★		★
	★		★

A golden influence has caused this dream; do not ignore it.

★			★
★	★		★
★	★	★	★
	★		★
	★		★

A dream of universal character indicating troubles to many powerful persons.

★			★
★		★	★
★	★	★	★
	★		★
	★		★

You are warned to guard your actions after this dream.

★	★	★	★
★	★		★
	★		★
★	★	★	★
	★		★

A frightful dream you have had, but its omens are happy.

★	★	★	★
	★	★	★
	★		★
★	★	★	★
	★		★

You will shortly take a journey; prepare.

★			★
★	★		★
★	★	★	★
	★		★
★	★	★	★

Soon you will hear of illness or the death of a loved one.

★			★
	★	★	★
★	★	★	★
	★		★
★	★	★	★

Grief is here forecast.

Hieroglyphic Emblem

```
                    ★   ★
                    ★   ★
                    ★   ★
                     ★
                    ★   ★
```

Sign 1	Sign 2	**CANCER**
★ ★ ★ ★ ★ ★ ★ ★ ★	★ ★ ★ ★ ★ ★ ★ ★ ★	An unimportant dream unless it concerns money, in which case it shows deceit.
★ ★ ★ ★ ★ ★ ★ ★ ★ ★	★ ★ ★ ★ ★ ★ ★ ★ ★	An omen that you will travel or hear news of a traveller.
★ ★ ★ ★ ★	★ ★ ★ ★ ★ ★	Melancholy and affliction are here denoted.
★ ★ ★ ★ ★ ★	★ ★ ★ ★ ★	You will hear news of a death.
★ ★ ★ ★ ★ ★ ★	★ ★ ★ ★ ★ ★ ★ ★	Aches and pains are predicted for the dreamer.
★ ★ ★ ★ ★ ★ ★ ★	★ ★ ★ ★ ★ ★ ★	Sickness and trouble are here forecast.
★ ★ ★ ★ ★ ★ ★	★ ★ ★ ★ ★ ★	Enemies over whom you will triumph are near at hand.

A dream ominous of consternation and harsh words.

To a dark person this dream predicts many friends.

Mirth and cheer; be happy while you can.

An ill dream; you are warned to be watchful.

Beware of a sudden foe and you will conquer him.

You are warned to be on the lookout for trouble, sadness, heaviness, cares.

On the 1st day of the moon this dream foretells letters, on the 4th or 6th joy, on the 13th a funeral, on other days, sorrow.

Expect glad news after this dream.

★		★		Beware of secret and treacherous foes.
★	★	★	★	
★	★	★	★	
	★	★	★	
★	★	★	★	

★		★		Disappointments; you will not take the
★	★	★	★	journey you have planned.
★	★	★	★	
★	★	★		
★		★		

★		★		Sorrow is at hand.
★	★	★	★	
★	★	★	★	
	★	★	★	
★		★		

★	★	★	★	Travelling and many journeys are
	★	★		foretold.
	★	★		
	★	★	★	
★	★	★	★	

★	★	★	★	First a journey is forecast, next a voyage
	★	★		and dealings with sailors.
	★	★		
★	★	★		
★	★	★	★	

★		★		A treacherous dream, albeit it may have
★	★	★	★	been a happy one.
	★	★		
★		★	★	
★		★		

★		★		Beware, a treacherous woman may cost
★	★	★	★	you dear.
★		★		
★	★	★		
★		★		

★	★	★	★	An amazingly fortunate dream.
	★	★		
	★	★		
	★	★	★	
	★	★		

★ ★ ★ ★	A favourable dream, predicting money or letters by messengers.
★ ★	
★ ★	
★ ★ ★	
★ ★	

A favourable dream, predicting money or letters by messengers.

Annoyances and differences between friends.

A dream warning you of approaching illness.

One of your undertakings will fail.

A fortunate dream denoting rich and powerful friends.

Many moons of prosperity and good fortune will follow this dream.

Disappointments are here signified.

Losses and business worries are foretold.

 This dream is an index of much diversity.

Hieroglyphic Emblem

Sign

1	2	SATURN
★★ ★★		You will soon attend a funeral.
★★ ★★		An ominous sign denoting the death of your dearest friend.
★ ★		You shall have difficulty in obtaining that for which you strive.
★ ★		Sepulchres, biers and funerals are here indicated.
★★ ★★		Merry-making, feasts and dancing are here augured.

173

★ ★ ★ ★	Friendship is promised through this dream.

Friendship is promised through this dream.

The dreamer is hereby warned against anger.

The expected shall not come to pass.

Joy and profit though letters and books.

Legacies and gain through the dead are here predicted.

You are warned of deceit in one to whom you have shown courtesy.

Concealed feelings are indicated by this dream.

A good omen of fortune soon to visit the dreamer.

★ ★ ★ ★				Your thought and your dream are contrasting.

★ ★				Something which you have lately sought shall be accomplished without labour.

★ ★				The dream warns you against signing documents.

★ ★ ★ ★				You will shortly receive a large inheritance.

★ ★ ★ ★				New friends and a turn in the tide of good fortune.

★ ★				The attentions of fair and kind women.

★ ★				Letters telling of love and courtship.

★ ★				Safety in the midst of difficulties.

175

★		★		Riding on horseback and travelling
★		★		swiftly.
★	★	★	★	
★	★	★	★	
★	★	★		

★		★		Changes, removals, voyages.
★	★	★	★	
★	★	★	★	
★		★		
★		★	★	

★		★		An unlucky dream of thwarted
★	★	★	★	desires.
★	★	★	★	
★		★		
★	★	★		

★	★	★	★	A dream of riches.
★		★		
★	★	★	★	
★		★		
★		★	★	

★	★	★	★	A prosperous fortune awaits you,
★		★		persevere.
★	★	★	★	
★		★		
★	★	★		

★		★		Losses and financial difficulties.
★	★	★	★	
★		★		
★	★	★	★	
★		★	★	

★		★		An omen of thieves; guard your
★	★	★	★	home.
★		★		
★	★	★	★	
★	★	★		

★	★	★	★	Tidings, letters and messages.
★		★		
★		★		
★	★	★	★	
★		★	★	

★ ★ ★ ★
  ★   ★
  ★   ★
★ ★ ★ ★
★ ★ ★
	Except on Sunday this dream predicts money.

★   ★
  ★   ★
★ ★ ★ ★
  ★   ★
★ ★ ★
	Avoid quarrelling and watch your words well.

★   ★
  ★   ★
★ ★ ★ ★
  ★   ★
  ★ ★ ★
	A sign predicting red-haired friends of whom you should beware.

Hieroglyphic Emblem ★
     ★ ★
     ★ ★
     ★ ★
     ★ ★

Sign

1	2	**LEO**
★ ★ ★ ★ ★ ★ ★ ★ ★ ★ ★ ★ ★ ★ ★ ★ ★ ★ ★		Bounteous favours of fortune are here predicted.
★ ★ ★ ★ ★ ★ ★ ★ ★ ★ ★ ★ ★ ★ ★ ★ ★ ★ ★		Profit through merchandise or from overseas.

★   ★ ★
  ★   ★
  ★   ★
  ★   ★
  ★   ★
		Letters, news and gifts.

```
★ ★     ★
  ★     ★
  ★     ★
  ★     ★
  ★     ★
```
The dreamer will shortly find a true, kind friend.

```
★ ★     ★
★ ★ ★ ★
  ★     ★
  ★     ★
  ★     ★
```
Friends are here forecast and to the businessman, money.

```
  ★   ★ ★
★ ★ ★ ★
  ★     ★
  ★     ★
  ★     ★
```
This dream forecasts marriage within the year.

```
  ★   ★ ★
  ★     ★
  ★     ★
★ ★ ★ ★
★ ★ ★ ★
```
Great disappointment in one of your undertakings which shall fail.

```
★ ★     ★
  ★     ★
  ★     ★
★ ★ ★ ★
★ ★ ★ ★
```
Peril if you travel after this dream, also trouble and loss through writings and papers.

```
★ ★     ★
★ ★ ★ ★
  ★     ★
★ ★ ★ ★
★ ★ ★ ★
```
Be warned against legal action and confusion amongst papers.

```
  ★   ★ ★
★ ★ ★ ★
  ★     ★
★ ★ ★ ★
★ ★ ★ ★
```
If dreamed on the third day of the moon, death of blood relatives.

```
★ ★     ★
  ★     ★
★ ★ ★ ★
★ ★ ★ ★
★ ★ ★ ★
```
A warning against secret enemies.

				Predicts mastery over secret opponents.
★		★	★	
★			★	
★	★	★	★	
★	★	★	★	
★	★	★	★	

				The revival of a past grievance long forgotten by the dreamer.
★	★		★	
★	★	★	★	
★	★	★	★	
	★		★	
★	★	★	★	

				Beware of losses.
★		★	★	
★	★	★	★	
★	★	★	★	
	★		★	
★	★	★	★	

				Death of some of your family.
★	★		★	
★	★	★	★	
★	★	★	★	
★	★	★	★	
	★		★	

				The dreamer will shortly attend the funeral of a loved one.
★		★	★	
★	★	★	★	
★	★	★	★	
★	★	★	★	
	★		★	

				Beware of signing documents.
★	★		★	
	★		★	
	★		★	
	★		★	
★	★	★	★	

				Probable loss through thieves.
	★	★	★	
	★		★	
	★		★	
	★		★	
★	★	★	★	

				Avoid the quarrels denoted by this dream.
	★	★	★	
	★		★	
	★		★	
★	★	★	★	
	★		★	

★　★　　　★
　★　　　　★
　★　　　　★
★　★　　★　★
　★　　　　★

You will be angered by letters or papers.

★　★　　　★
★　★　　★　★
★　★　　★　★
　★　　　　★
　★　　　　★

Restlessness and change.

　★　　　★　★
★　★　　★　★
★　★　　★　★
　★　　　　★
　★　　　　★

Sad news causing dismay and sorrow.

　★　　　★　★
　★　　　　★
★　★　　★　★
★　★　　★　★
　★　　　　★

Deceitful friends and thoughtless persons will cause you trouble.

★　★　　　★
　★　　　　★
★　★　　★　★
★　★　　★　★
　★　　　　★

Anger, strife and ill news are here betokened.

★　★　　　★
　★　　　　★
★　★　　★　★
　★　　　　★
　★　　　　★

A speedy change for the better in your fortunes.

　★　　　★　★
　★　　　　★
★　★　　★　★
　★　　　　★
　★　　　　★

Good news from friends.

　★　　　★　★
★　★　　★　★
　★　　　　★
★　★　　★　★
　★　　　　★

Losses and sorrow are approaching.

A secret enemy would wish to harm you.

However evil this dream may appear it augurs good.

Changes, journeys, possibly across water.

News of a woman friend and from one in trouble.

A journey is here foretold.

Hieroglyphic Emblem

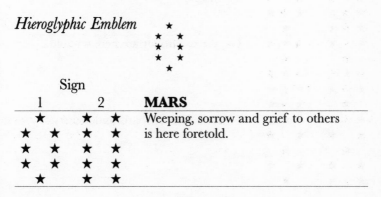

Sign

1   2   **MARS**

Weeping, sorrow and grief to others is here foretold.

181

Dictionary of Dreams

★	★		★	A relative in a far distant land will be laid to rest.
★	★	★	★	
★	★	★	★	
★	★	★	★	
★	★		★	
	★		★ ★	On Monday or Wednesday the dream implies good; otherwise unimportant.
★	★	★		Travelling and a long journey are forecast.
★	★	★		A good dream auguring plentiful wealth.
	★	★ ★		You shall receive gifts and favours.
	★	★ ★		In three weeks you shall make an acquaintance who will become a true friend.
★	★	★		Happiness and joy are here foretold.
★	★	★		Business, letters, charts and activity of mind.

182

★		★	★
★	★	★	★
★		★	
★	★	★	★
★		★	★

Trouble through a dark woman.

★	★		★
★			★
★	★	★	★
★	★	★	★
★		★	

A deceitful dream! Beware of a red-haired man.

★		★	★
★		★	
★	★	★	★
★	★	★	★
★		★	

You will shortly hear of the illness of a friend.

★	★		★
★	★	★	★
★	★	★	★
★		★	
★	★	★	

The perils that of late have troubled the dreamer will vanish; his destiny will mend.

★		★	★
★	★	★	★
★	★	★	★
★		★	
★		★	★

Grief and sorrow are here implied.

★	★		★
★	★	★	★
★	★	★	★
★	★	★	★
★		★	★

A mixture of joy and sorrow is here predicted.

★		★	★
★	★	★	★
★	★	★	★
★	★	★	★
★	★	★	

Tears and annoyances, followed by joy.

★		★	★
★	★	★	★
★		★	
★		★	
★		★	★

You will either be married yourself or will attend a wedding.

★ ★ · ★ ★ ★ ★ ★ · ★ · ★ · ★ · ★ ★ ★ · ★	On the 7th day of the moon this dream forecasts a journey; on any other day, new friends.
· ★ · ★ ★ · ★ · ★ · ★ · ★ ★ ★ ★ ★ · ★ · ★ ★	Disputes in relation to writings.
★ ★ · ★ · ★ · ★ · ★ · ★ ★ ★ ★ ★ ★ ★ · ★	A sudden death is predicted.
· ★ · ★ ★ · ★ · ★ · ★ · ★ · ★ · ★ ★ ★ · ★	Trouble will follow this dream.
★ ★ · ★ · ★ · ★ · ★ · ★ · ★ · ★ · ★ ★ ★	Cares will beset the dreamer.
★ ★ · ★ ★ ★ ★ ★ ★ ★ ★ ★ · ★ · ★ · ★ ★ ★	Disappointments, relating to money.
· ★ · ★ ★ ★ ★ ★ ★ ★ ★ ★ ★ · ★ · ★ ★ ★ · ★	Deferred hope.
· ★ · ★ ★ · ★ · ★ ★ ★ ★ ★ ★ ★ ★ ★ ★ ★ · ★	Good fortune will soon follow this vision.

184

★ ★ ★ ★ ★ ★ ★ ★ ★ ★ ★ ★ ★ ★ ★ ★	To a female this dream signifies marriage; to a male it signifies deceit.
★ ★ ★ ★ ★ ★ ★ ★ ★ ★ ★ ★ ★ ★	An omen of many months of good fortune.
★ ★ ★ ★ ★ ★ ★ ★ ★ ★ ★ ★ ★ ★	Harsh words concerning money.
★ ★ ★ ★ ★ ★ ★ ★ ★ ★ ★ ★ ★ ★	The receipt of money.
★ ★ ★ ★ ★ ★ ★ ★ ★ ★ ★ ★ ★ ★	Unexpected news.
★ ★ ★ ★ ★ ★ ★ ★ ★ ★ ★ ★ ★ ★ ★ ★ ★	An unimportant dream.
★ ★ ★ ★ ★ ★ ★ ★ ★ ★ ★ ★ ★ ★ ★ ★ ★	Let the dreamer prepare for a removal unless dreamt at the full moon.

Hieroglyphic Emblem

Sign				VIRGO
1		2		

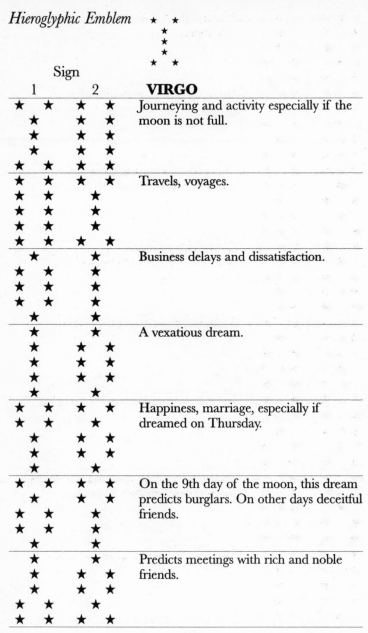

★ ★	★ ★	Journeying and activity especially if the moon is not full.
★	★ ★	
★	★ ★	
★	★ ★	
★ ★	★ ★	
★ ★	★ ★	Travels, voyages.
★ ★	★	
★ ★	★	
★ ★	★	
★ ★	★ ★	
★	★	Business delays and dissatisfaction.
★ ★	★	
★ ★	★	
★ ★	★	
★	★	
★	★	A vexatious dream.
★	★ ★	
★	★ ★	
★	★ ★	
★	★	
★ ★	★ ★	Happiness, marriage, especially if dreamed on Thursday.
★ ★	★	
★	★ ★	
★	★ ★	
★	★	
★ ★	★ ★	On the 9th day of the moon, this dream predicts burglars. On other days deceitful friends.
★	★ ★	
★ ★	★	
★ ★	★	
★	★	
★	★	Predicts meetings with rich and noble friends.
★	★ ★	
★	★ ★	
★ ★	★	
★ ★	★ ★	

★ ★ ★ ★ ★ ★ ★ ★ ★ ★ ★ ★ ★ ★ ★	Predicts the fulfilment of desires and intentions.
★ ★ ★ ★ ★ ★ ★ ★ ★ ★ ★ ★ ★ ★ ★ ★ ★	Riches after poverty; fulfilment of wishes.
★ ★ ★ ★ ★ ★ ★ ★ ★ ★ ★ ★ ★ ★ ★ ★ ★	Honours and influence over others will come to you after this dream.
★ ★ ★ ★ ★ ★ ★ ★ ★ ★ ★ ★ ★ ★ ★ ★ ★	On a Friday this is an unlucky dream, otherwise unimportant.
★ ★ ★ ★ ★ ★ ★ ★ ★ ★ ★ ★ ★ ★ ★ ★ ★	Favours, presents and benefits from wealthy persons.
★ ★ ★ ★ ★ ★ ★ ★ ★ ★ ★ ★ ★ ★ ★ ★ ★	Travels or flitting from place to place.
★ ★ ★ ★ ★ ★ ★ ★ ★ ★ ★ ★ ★ ★ ★ ★ ★	To a single female marriage, to others the buying of houses or heavy goods.
★ ★ ★ ★ ★ ★ ★ ★ ★ ★ ★ ★ ★ ★ ★	Delay in the marriage of a friend.

Marriage, joyful news, the desires of your heart.

Hatred, joy and sorrow combined.

Secret enemies especially a dark taciturn person.

A good dream for a sick person; on the increase of the moon it foretells the coming of money.

A reward for that which you have done.

Subjugation to the rich, profit to the poor are here indicated.

Crosses in love are here forecast.

Danger even death to the sick; to one in captivity or grief, a speedy release.

Sickness through over-indulgence.

Merry-making, joy, new clothes.

A dream forecasting happiness and prosperity.

Fortunate and happy except on the full of the moon.

A long peaceful life is promised.

You are warned against deceitful friends.

Quarrelling and angry words.

A bad dream, guard your actions.

★		★		Sickness either to yourself or to family.
	★		★	★
★	★		★	
	★		★	★
★	★		★	★

Hieroglyphic Emblem

	Sign		
1		2		**MERCURY**

★		★	★	On Friday this predicts marriage to
★	★	★	★	the young and success to the aged.
	★	★	★	
	★	★	★	
	★	★	★	

★	★		★	A long journey with a satisfactory
★	★	★	★	ending.
★	★	★		
★	★	★		
★	★	★		

	★	★	★	Sorrows and care surround you.
	★	★		
	★	★	★	
	★	★	★	
	★	★	★	

★	★		★	An enemy will endeavour to harm the
	★		★	dreamer.
★	★	★		
★	★	★		
★	★	★		

★	★		★	Wealth and plenty in your old age.
★	★	★	★	
	★	★	★	
	★	★	★	
	★	★	★	

In a few years time you will have fortune and prosperity.

You will gain wealth but you may then lose it.

A present of gold and silver.

Riches in later life.

Poverty for a while through the dreamer's own negligence.

A dream of trouble in high places, in affairs of state, etc.

A dream warning you to examine your character in case you are discredited.

Trouble and sadness after merry-making.

You will shortly find a sincere and trustworthy friend.

Beware of robbery; a heavy loss is predicted.

Here are shown rides on horseback and travels.

Worrying removals or voyages.

Great evil if your dream falls on a Saturday.

An evil minded enemy, but with care you will be victorious.

Financial success and health are here indicated.

Many enemies against whom you must guard.

★ ★   ★
   ★   ★
★ ★   ★
★ ★   ★
   ★   ★ ★

On Friday the 13th of the month this dream foretells death amongst your relatives; otherwise insignificant.

★ ★   ★
   ★   ★
★   ★ ★
★   ★ ★
★   ★ ★

Celebrations and prosperity.

★   ★ ★
   ★   ★
★ ★   ★
★ ★   ★
★ ★   ★

Wealth and success to the dreamer.

★ ★   ★
★ ★ ★ ★
★ ★   ★
   ★   ★ ★
   ★   ★ ★

Profit and honour.

★   ★ ★
★ ★ ★ ★
   ★   ★ ★
★ ★   ★
★ ★   ★

Beware of horned cattle and four-footed beasts.

★ ★   ★
★ ★ ★ ★
   ★   ★ ★
★ ★   ★
   ★   ★ ★

Letters containing news of absent friends.

★   ★ ★
★ ★ ★ ★
★ ★   ★
   ★   ★ ★
★ ★   ★

Illness hovers near the dreamer.

★ ★   ★
   ★   ★
   ★   ★ ★
★ ★   ★
   ★   ★ ★

Much walking or travelling.

193

★		★	★	News and financial affairs.
	★		★	
★	★		★	
	★		★	★
★	★		★	

★	★		★	An evil dream denoting temporary
	★		★	poverty.
	★		★	★
★	★		★	
★	★		★	

	★		★	★	Beware of removals and changes after
	★		★		this dream.
★	★		★	
	★		★	★
	★		★	★

Hieroglyphic Emblem

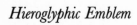

LIBRA

★		★	★	You are warned of danger from thieves
★		★	★	and burglars.
★		★	★	
★	★	★	★	
★		★	★	

★	★		★	Fair persons will profit you much.
★	★		★	
★	★		★	
★	★	★	★	
★	★		★	

★		★	★	You may expect visitors from a long
★		★	★	journey.
★		★	★	
★		★		
★		★	★	

A fortunate dream; you will receive money through letters and packets.

Many months of fortune and prosperity.

Profitable business and increase thereof.

Guard against a spiteful enemy who would harm you financially.

Be prepared for sudden and sad news.

Confusion among workmen and labourers from which you may suffer.

Some secret foe has lately been working mischief with your name. Take care.

Beware of deceit and false friends.

```
  ★      ★  ★      To a male this dream indicates trouble
★   ★      ★        with a female.
  ★      ★  ★
★   ★    ★  ★
  ★      ★  ★
```

```
  ★      ★  ★      Better fortune is at hand; your troubles
★   ★      ★        will soon pass.
★   ★      ★
★   ★    ★  ★
★   ★      ★
```

```
★   ★      ★      You will receive a gift of money and will
  ★      ★  ★      prosper generally.
  ★      ★  ★
★   ★    ★  ★
  ★      ★  ★
```

```
  ★      ★  ★      A journey or removal within six months.
★   ★      ★
★   ★      ★
★   ★    ★  ★
  ★      ★  ★
```

```
★   ★      ★      Misfortunes and troubles are here
  ★      ★  ★      foretold.
  ★      ★  ★
★   ★    ★  ★
★   ★      ★
```

```
★   ★      ★      A change is here predicted.
  ★      ★  ★
  ★      ★  ★
  ★        ★
★   ★      ★
```

```
  ★      ★  ★      A funeral in the family which will grieve
★   ★      ★        you sorely.
★   ★      ★
  ★        ★
  ★      ★  ★
```

```
  ★      ★  ★      To a male this signifies approaching
★   ★      ★        nuptials, to a female courtship.
  ★      ★  ★
  ★        ★
  ★      ★  ★
```

On a Thursday, Tuesday or Wednesday, good fortune and success to the dreamer.

Losses; avoid speculation.

Sorrow; also guard your health against sickness.

Luck will attend you in six weeks.

You should warn your absent friends to beware of approaching trouble.

Wealth and fortune to the dreamer, death to his enemies.

Unimportant; a mixture of good and evil.

Love and happiness; prosperity and marriage among your family.

			You have just escaped loss and sickness.

			Fortunate on a Sunday; otherwise look for a month of troubles and vexations.

			Toil, worry and anxiety are here forecast.

			An unimportant dream due to ill-health.

			New friends are here forecast.

Hieroglyphic Emblem

Sign			
1	2		**VENUS**
			A sad dream denoting sorrows and cares.

198

★	★		★		Trouble among your absent friends.
★	★		★		
★	★		★		
★	★		★		
★	★	★	★		

	★		★	★	Many changes in your life.
	★		★	★	
	★		★	★	
	★		★	★	
	★		★		

★	★		★	Troubles and cares will befall you for
★	★		★	a short time.
★	★		★	
★	★		★	
	★		★	

★	★		★		Joy and merry-making.
★	★		★		
	★		★	★
	★		★	★
	★		★	

	★		★	★	First disappointment, then the receipt
	★		★	★	of a large sum of money.
★	★		★	
★	★		★	
	★		★	

	★		★	★	If dreamed on Sunday and the 10th
	★		★	★	day of the moon, this dream denotes
	★		★	★	wealth in middle age.
★	★		★	
★	★	★	★	

★	★		★		An enemy of the dreamer will shortly
★	★		★		die.
★	★		★		
	★		★	★
★	★	★	★	

★	★		★		You will soon see someone whom you
★	★		★		have sorely missed.
	★		★	★
★	★		★	
★	★	★	★	

★		★	★	Seven months of trouble will follow
★		★	★	this dream.
★	★		★	
★		★	★	
★	★	★	★	

★	★		★	Anger, strife, loss through treachery.
★		★	★	
★	★		★	
★	★		★	
★	★	★	★	

★		★	★	Unless your dream proceeds from ill-
★	★		★	health, beware of a dark person near
★		★	★	you.
★		★	★	
★	★	★	★	

★		★	★	A fortunate dream.
★	★	★		
★	★	★		
★	★	★		
★	★	★	★	

★	★		★	You will soon take a long and prosperous
★		★	★	journey.
★		★	★	
★		★	★	
★	★	★	★	

★		★	★	Marriage and love are here signified.
★	★	★		
★		★	★	
★		★	★	
★		★		

★	★		★	Treachery is here denoted.
★		★	★	
★	★	★		
★	★	★		
★		★		

★		★	★	Beware of a faithless friend who will
★		★	★	slander you.
★		★	★	
★	★	★		
★		★		

A warning not to enter your enemy's home.

The present weariness and care will soon change to better fortunes.

The death of a dear friend or relative who lives at a distance.

Good fortune, gifts of money, joyful letters.

Heavy cares, yet victory over adversaries at last.

Business cares and disappointments.

After three days the dreamer will escape harm.

Success in business; joy and pleasure.

★ ★ ★ ★ ★ ★ ★ ★ ★ ★ ★ ★ ★ ★	A dream that bodes well for public life and for voyages.
★ ★ ★ ★ ★ ★ ★ ★ ★ ★ ★ ★ ★ ★ ★ ★	Troubles that will soon pass.
★ ★ ★ ★ ★ ★ ★ ★ ★ ★ ★ ★ ★ ★ ★ ★	A warning not to be too confiding in your friends.
★ ★ ★ ★ ★ ★ ★ ★ ★ ★ ★ ★ ★ ★	Beware of journeys or voyages for the space of one moon.
★ ★ ★ ★ ★ ★ ★ ★ ★ ★ ★ ★ ★ ★	This dream foretells a sudden rise in fortunes.
★ ★ ★ ★ ★ ★ ★ ★ ★ ★ ★ ★ ★ ★ ★ ★	Prepare your mourning dress, someone is about to die.
★ ★ ★ ★ ★ ★ ★ ★ ★ ★ ★ ★ ★ ★ ★ ★	A warning to look to your health.

Hieroglyphic Emblem ★ ★
★
★
★
★

	Sign			
1		2		**SCORPIO**
★ ★		★	★	Predicts a joyous time; financial success beyond present expectation.
★		★	★	
★		★	★	
★		★	★	
★		★	★	
★ ★		★	★	Changing circumstances, money, friends and happiness.
★ ★		★		
★ ★		★		
★ ★		★		
★ ★		★		
★		★		A beneficial, happy voyage.
★		★	★	
★		★	★	
★		★	★	
★		★	★	
★		★		An unimportant dream.
★ ★		★		
★ ★		★		
★ ★		★		
★ ★		★		
★ ★		★	★	Your fortunes will improve, but for the present avoid speculation.
★ ★		★		
★		★	★	
★		★	★	
★		★	★	
★ ★		★	★	A faithless friend will harm the dreamer.
★		★	★	
★ ★		★		
★ ★		★		
★ ★		★		
★		★		Victory over adversaries who shall rise up against you.
★		★	★	
★		★	★	
★ ★		★		
★ ★		★		

203

A warning of sickness; guard your health.

News from distant friends or from one whom you have believed dead.

Financial success; plentiful gold and silver.

A warning to beware of the law and lawyers.

Your desire shall be fulfilled.

You shall acquire a small sum, but do not risk it in speculation, in case you lose.

Happy surprises are here implied.

Take care whom you consult on important matters.

Interpretation of Dreams

★ ★ ★ ★ ★ ★ ★ ★ ★ ★ ★ ★ ★ ★	A dream of funerals, grief and cares.
★ ★ ★ ★ ★ ★ ★ ★ ★ ★ ★ ★ ★ ★	A joyous dream; you will be invited to many celebrations.
★ ★ ★ ★ ★ ★ ★ ★ ★ ★ ★ ★ ★ ★	To the young this brings joy and celebration; to the aged the peace they desire.
★ ★ ★ ★ ★ ★ ★ ★ ★ ★ ★ ★ ★ ★	To a female this dream signifies romance and possible marriage.
★ ★ ★ ★ ★ ★ ★ ★ ★ ★ ★ ★ ★ ★	Take care in case you make an enemy who will cost you dear.
★ ★ ★ ★ ★ ★ ★ ★ ★ ★ ★ ★ ★ ★ ★ ★	Victory over an adversary.
★ ★ ★ ★ ★ ★ ★ ★ ★ ★ ★ ★ ★ ★ ★ ★	Beware of scandals which are being circulated about you.
★ ★ ★ ★ ★ ★ ★ ★ ★ ★ ★ ★ ★ ★	An illness within three weeks is here predicted.

Sorrow and pain; the death of a near relative.

An unimportant dream.

A quiet, unimportant dream.

A change in fortune; prosperity, happiness, pleasure.

You will shortly receive news and letters containing money.

Unfavourable conditions will cause misfortunes for a time.

A funeral if dreamed on the 4th, 5th or 20th day of the month.

Quarrelling and strife.

1		2		
★ ★	★ ★			Your best friend will shortly be in trouble and will seek your aid.
★ ★	★			
★	★ ★			
★	★ ★			
★ ★	★			

Hieroglyphic Emblem

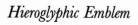

	Sign		
1		2	**PALLAS**
★ ★	★ ★		An unfortunate dream; worse on the new moon.
★ ★	★ ★		
★ ★	★ ★		
★	★ ★		
★	★ ★		
★ ★	★ ★		Beware of crossing water after this dream.
★ ★	★ ★		
★ ★	★ ★		
★ ★	★		
★ ★	★		
★	★		Changes and perplexities are here indicated.
★	★		
★	★		
★	★ ★		
★	★ ★		
★	★		A dream of vain toil and labour.
★	★		
★	★		
★ ★	★		
★ ★	★		
★ ★	★ ★		Wealth and plenty; success financially and in love.
★ ★	★ ★		
★	★		
★	★ ★		
★	★ ★		

★	★	★	★
★	★	★	★
	★		★
★	★	★	
★	★	★	

Joy, health and wealth amongst your relatives.

★	★	★	★
	★		★
★	★	★	★
★	★	★	
★	★	★	

Guard yourself and your house against thieves.

★	★	★	★
	★		★
★	★	★	★
	★	★	★
	★	★	★

To the sick, danger of death; to the well, care and grief.

★	★	★	★
★	★	★	★
★	★	★	★
	★	★	★
★	★		★

An evil dream, financial cares and crosses in love.

★	★	★	★
★	★	★	★
★	★	★	★
★	★		★
	★		★	★

An omen of sore affliction.

★			★
★	★	★	★
★	★	★	★
★	★		★
★	★		★

A dream forecasting bad weather.

★			★
★	★	★	★
★	★	★	★
	★	★	★
	★	★	★

A dream of hope, but do not be too confident.

★			★
★	★	★	★
★	★	★	★
★	★		★
	★		★	★

On the 1st day of the moon, a journey; on the 3rd day a friend; on any other day deceit.

A dream signifying that your mind is unnecessarily burdened with fears and troubles, but with care you need not fear.

A dream signifying long journeys which will benefit the dreamer.

Strange news will alarm the dreamer.

A dream of joy and marriage festivals.

This dream denotes the passing of evil times and the beginning of a new era.

An omen of secret enemies; beware of treachery and deceit.

Put your trust in no one; many would harm you if they could.

Difficult business dealings, deliberations and action.

Success in law or finance.

Voyages, journeys, the meeting with absent friends.

Your dream is an omen of war, pestilence and famine.

Beware of enemies; trust few whom you know.

Disappointment in business, troubles in love.

Crosses to the lover, disappointments to the business man.

A dream warning you of the loss of goods and money.

Money and a change in your fortune for the better.

★ ★ ★ ★	Falsehood and treachery, but in three
★ ★	days you will have good news.
★ ★ ★ ★	
★ ★ ★	
★ ★ ★	

★ ★ ★ ★	Writings, study, letters and books are
★ ★ ★ ★	here denoted.
★ ★	
★ ★ ★	
★ ★ ★	

★ ★ ★ ★	Danger from the sea is here prophesied.
★ ★ ★ ★	
★ ★	
★ ★ ★	
★ ★ ★	

Hieroglyphic Emblem

Sign			
1		2	**SAGITTARIUS**
★	★ ★		A dream of prosperity and fortune.
★	★ ★		
★ ★ ★ ★			
★ ★ ★ ★			
★ ★ ★ ★			

★ ★ ★	Trouble on Saturday, money when
★ ★ ★	dreamed on other days.
★ ★ ★ ★	
★ ★ ★ ★	
★ ★ ★ ★	

★ ★ ★	Changes, travel, journeys.
★ ★ ★	
★ ★	
★ ★	
★ ★	

★ ★ ★ Removals and changes.
★ ★ ★
  ★ ★
  ★ ★
  ★ ★

  ★ ★ ★ On the 5th, 8th or 12th day of the moon
  ★ ★ ★ this vision denotes funerals.
  ★ ★
★ ★ ★ ★
★ ★ ★ ★

★ ★ ★ A fortunate dream financially.
★ ★ ★
  ★ ★
★ ★ ★ ★
★ ★ ★ ★

★ ★ ★ A dream betokening grief, sadness
  ★ ★ ★ anxiety.
★ ★ ★ ★
★ ★ ★ ★
★ ★ ★ ★

  ★ ★ ★ Sickness is shadowing you or your
  ★ ★ ★ household.
★ ★ ★ ★
★ ★ ★ ★
★ ★ ★ ★

★ ★ ★ You will be in jeopardy.
★ ★ ★
★ ★ ★ ★
  ★ ★
★ ★ ★ ★

  ★ ★ ★ Losses, crosses and afflictions threaten.
  ★ ★ ★
★ ★ ★ ★
  ★ ★
★ ★ ★ ★

★ ★ ★ Sadness and care are here denoted.
★ ★ ★
★ ★ ★ ★
★ ★ ★ ★
  ★ ★

Much walking and riding on horseback.

Evil news is here foretold.

One whom you have loved and trusted will become your enemy.

The arrival of letters and of a friend long absent.

A vexatious happening is here foretold.

Pleasure, fortune and a wedding amongst your family.

Pleasure and happiness in your domestic affairs.

Anger is here foretold.

An omen of a journey or a removal in a few weeks.

Beware of bodily hurt or injury from an animal.

You have a secret foe in a tall, taciturn person.

Good fortune, a plentiful supply of money.

An omen of legal action which the dreamer should avoid.

Do not be disheartened by delay; your wishes will finally be attained.

Wealth through trade or merchandise.

An omen of danger during the present moon; avoid the water.

★ ★ ★ ★ ★ ★ ★ ★ ★ ★ ★ ★ ★ ★	Celebration, joy and mirth are here foretold.
★ ★ ★ ★ ★ ★ ★ ★ ★ ★ ★ ★ ★ ★ ★ ★	Abundance, peace and happiness.
★ ★ ★ ★ ★ ★ ★ ★ ★ ★ ★ ★ ★ ★ ★ ★	This dream forecasts legal trouble, guard against theft.
★ ★ ★ ★ ★ ★ ★ ★ ★ ★ ★ ★ ★ ★ ★ ★	Your dream warns you of disgrace; it would be wise to take care.
★ ★ ★ ★ ★ ★ ★ ★ ★ ★ ★ ★ ★ ★ ★ ★	A happy life and good fortune are here predicted.

Hieroglyphic Emblem

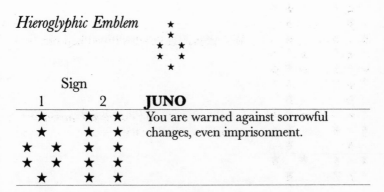

Sign

1	2	**JUNO**
★ ★ ★ ★ ★ ★ ★ ★ ★ ★ ★ ★ ★ ★ ★ ★ ★	You are warned against sorrowful changes, even imprisonment.

| | | | This indicates the death of some friends to whom you are deeply attached. |

| | | | Within three months you will lose one whom you love. |

| | | | This forecasts unprofitable removals. |

| | | | Many of your undertakings will prove unprofitable and troublesome. |

| | | | You are warned of ill-health, also of a deceitful friend near you. |

| | | | Sickness to yourself and idle words about you. |

| | | | Privation, loss, disappointment. |

| | | | On the 9th day of the moon this dream forecasts theft and cheating. |

★   ★ ★   Beware of some curious accident which
★   ★ ★   will befall you.
 ★   ★
★ ★ ★ ★
 ★   ★ ★

★ ★   ★   To a female an offer of marriage; to a
 ★   ★ ★   male angry words.
★ ★ ★ ★
★ ★ ★ ★
★ ★   ★

 ★   ★ ★   Trouble and harassment in the family.
★ ★   ★
★ ★ ★ ★
★ ★ ★ ★
 ★   ★ ★

★ ★   ★   This denotes the friendship of aged
★ ★   ★   persons.
★ ★ ★ ★
 ★   ★
★ ★   ★

 ★   ★ ★   Many are envious and oppose you, but
 ★   ★ ★   they cannot harm you.
★ ★ ★ ★
 ★   ★
 ★   ★ ★

★ ★   ★   Sorrow and misfortune are here denoted.
★ ★   ★
★ ★ ★ ★
★ ★ ★ ★
 ★   ★ ★

 ★   ★ ★   Poverty and misfortune are here forecast.
 ★   ★ ★
★ ★ ★ ★
★ ★ ★ ★
★ ★   ★

★ ★   ★   Deceit and slander surround you.
 ★   ★ ★
★ ★ ★ ★
★ ★ ★ ★
 ★   ★ ★

An unstable dream, caused by bad feeling.

A happy old age and an end to your afflictions is here forecast.

Prosperity governs this dream.

Increase, gain and wealth are hereby forecast.

Ominous of trouble through beautiful women.

Beware of false friends who betray and slander you.

Avoid the water after this vision.

Evil if dreamed on Friday, denoting deferred hopes.

★ ★ ★		To a female this denotes love letters; it warns a male against improper women.

★ ★ ★		Pleasure comes after pain.

★ ★ ★		The death of a neighbour is here forecast.

★ ★ ★		Ill-health and much sickness are here indicated.

★ ★ ★		You are warned of sickness near you.

★ ★ ★		Mourning and angry words from those with whom the dreamer comes in contact.

★ ★ ★		A warning against deceptive and vain hopes.

Hieroglyphic Emblem

	Sign		CAPRICORN
1	2		
★★	★ ★★		The interpretation of this dream is connected with the church or some religious friend whom you shall meet.
★★	★		Barter, exchange, the counting of money.
★★	★ ★★		You shall soon make great and noble acquaintances.
★★	★		Letters and news from those long absent.
★★	★		Slanders and lying reports are being circulated concerning you.
★★	★ ★★		Troubles, annoyances, an unsettled time.
★★	★ ★★		Health, wealth and happiness.

```
★   ★       ★
  ★         ★
  ★         ★
  ★       ★   ★
  ★       ★   ★
```
The dreamer will soon receive good news.

```
★   ★       ★
★   ★     ★   ★
  ★         ★
★   ★       ★
★   ★       ★
```
You are warned that your pleasure will cost you dear.

```
  ★       ★   ★
★   ★     ★   ★
  ★         ★
  ★       ★   ★
  ★       ★   ★
```
Weddings and festive gatherings.

```
★   ★       ★
  ★         ★
★   ★     ★   ★
★   ★       ★
★   ★       ★
```
Strife and anger; be cautious.

```
  ★       ★   ★
  ★         ★
★   ★     ★   ★
  ★       ★   ★
  ★       ★   ★
```
Your dream denotes sudden frights.

```
★   ★       ★
★   ★     ★   ★
★   ★     ★   ★
  ★       ★   ★
★   ★       ★
```
Guard your home against thieves.

```
  ★       ★   ★
★   ★     ★   ★
★   ★     ★   ★
★   ★       ★
  ★       ★   ★
```
Your dream foretells good news.

```
★   ★       ★
★   ★     ★   ★
★   ★     ★   ★
★   ★       ★
  ★       ★   ★
```
After this dream, humiliation and sorrow, if not disgrace, will be your lot.

Great distress of mind.

You will find comfort and solace after your trouble.

This dream indicates the death of an enemy.

Your dream borders on anger and is therefore vain.

Three things are here predicted, a strange guest, a letter and the departure of an enemy.

A dream of poverty and misfortune.

Good news is at hand.

On Friday this dream brings news; on Sunday money; Monday travelling; Tuesday quarrelling; other days strife.

★ ★　　★		On the 12th day of the moon this
★　　★		dream augurs a legacy; on Thursday and
★ ★　★ ★		Sunday money.
★　★ ★		
★　★ ★		

★　★ ★	Advancement after hard work.
★　★	
★ ★　★ ★	
★ ★　★	
★　★ ★	

★ ★　★	The arrival of a friend.
★　★	
★ ★　★ ★	
★　★ ★	
★ ★　★	

★　★ ★	Deceit and vain words.
★ ★　★ ★	
★　★	
★ ★　★	
★　★ ★	

★ ★　★	A dream of illness, guard your health.
★ ★　★ ★	
★　★	
★　★ ★	
★ ★　★	

★ ★　★	Trials are at hand, but later your fortune
★ ★　★ ★	will mend.
★　★	
★　★ ★	
★ ★　★	

★ ★　★	Bad news, especially if dreamed on
★　★	Monday.
★ ★　★ ★	
★ ★　★	
★　★ ★	

★　★ ★	Great labour and small profit are here
★　★	foretold.
★ ★　★ ★	
★　★ ★	
★ ★　★	

Hieroglyphic Emblem

	Sign			**CERES**
★ ★		★ ★		A fortunate dream.
★		★ ★		
★ ★		★ ★		
★		★ ★		
★		★ ★		
★ ★		★ ★		Money and health.
★ ★		★		
★ ★		★ ★		
★ ★		★		
★ ★		★		
★		★		A vain and useless dream.
★		★ ★		
★		★		
★		★ ★		
★		★ ★		
★		★		A change in the dreamer's fortune for the better.
★ ★		★		
★		★		
★ ★		★		
★ ★		★		
★		★		Rejoicings, feastings and pleasure.
★		★ ★		
★		★		
★ ★		★		
★ ★		★		
★		★		On a Monday your dream foretells a marriage among your friends; on other days gladness.
★ ★		★		
★		★		
★ ★		★ ★		
★		★ ★		
★ ★		★ ★		News and letters from friends.
★ ★		★		
★		★		
★ ★		★		
★ ★		★		

★	★	★	★	You will travel three times within a year.
	★	★	★	
	★		★	
	★	★	★	
	★	★	★	

★	★	★	★	Beware of false friends who would do
	★	★	★	you harm.
★	★	★	★	
★	★	★		
★	★	★		

★	★	★	★	Within a month you will lose a friend by
★	★		★	death.
★	★	★	★	
	★	★	★	
	★	★	★	

★	★	★	★	A spiteful enemy would harm you.
★	★	★		
★	★	★	★	
	★	★	★	
★	★	★		

★	★	★	★	Some months of sorrow are before you.
	★	★	★	
★	★	★	★	
★	★	★		
	★	★	★	

★	★	★	★	Losses unless you look well to your
★	★	★		money.
★	★	★	★	
★	★	★		
	★	★	★	

★	★	★	★	Little import attaches to this dream.
	★	★	★	
★	★	★	★	
	★	★	★	
★	★	★		

	★		★	The grief and restlessness that has
★	★		★	burdened you will now disappear.
★	★	★	★	
★	★	★		
★	★	★		

	The vanishing of fear is here denoted.
	Danger of falls and bruises.
	The death of a relative will grieve you within the year.
	Funerals and burial of the dead.
	Grief through the death of a friend in a foreign land.
	A dream of many interpretations, among them the augury of loss by thieves.
	On the even days of the moon (the 2nd, 4th, 6th, etc.) this dream foretells removing; on other days sorrows.
	Death of a spiteful enemy; nevertheless you will have troubles after this dream.

★   ★
★   ★   ★
★   ★
★   ★   ★
★   ★   ★

Weeping, tears and sorrow.

★   ★
★   ★   ★
★   ★   ★   ★
★   ★   ★
★   ★   ★

On Thursday this dream predicts a year of happiness, on other days fortune.

★   ★
★   ★   ★
★   ★   ★   ★
  ★   ★   ★
  ★   ★   ★

A combination of good and evil is this vision.

★   ★
★   ★   ★
★   ★   ★   ★
★   ★   ★
★   ★   ★

Heavy responsibilities and enmities.

★   ★
★   ★   ★
★   ★   ★   ★
  ★   ★   ★
★   ★   ★

On Saturday your dream is good, on any other day it signifies sorrow and trouble.

★   ★   ★   ★
  ★   ★   ★
  ★   ★
★   ★   ★
  ★   ★   ★

A large sum of money is on the way to you.

★   ★   ★   ★
★   ★   ★
  ★   ★
  ★   ★   ★
★   ★   ★

Good fortune awaits the dreamer, peace and plenty.

Hieroglyphic Emblem

Sign 1	Sign 2	AQUARIUS
★ ★ ★ 　★ ★ ★ 　★	★ ★ ★ ★ ★ ★ ★ ★ ★ ★	Your dream warns you of disappointment.
★ ★ ★ ★ ★ ★ ★ ★ ★ ★	★ ★ ★ ★ ★ ★ ★	Beware of going on, or in the water after this dream.
★ ★ ★ ★ ★	★ ★ ★ ★ ★ ★ ★ ★	Take care of your money; financial losses.
★ ★ ★ ★ ★ ★ ★ ★	★ ★ ★ ★ ★	Beware of those who would malign you.
★ ★ ★ ★ ★ ★ ★	★ ★ ★ ★ ★ ★ ★ ★	Some relatives or near neighbours are your enemies.
★ ★ ★ ★ ★ ★ ★ ★	★ ★ ★ ★ ★ ★ ★	On the 3rd day and 9th day of the month, an unfortunate dream, denoting treason and false counsellors.
★ ★ ★ ★ ★ ★ ★	★ ★ ★ ★ ★ ★ ★ ★	You are warned against false friends who would harm you.

			Hurry and confusion, probably voyages.

			An unsettled time, anxiety and trouble.

			An unfortunate dream forecasting grief.

			On Thursday a funeral is predicted; on other days news of the severe affliction of a friend.

			Good fortune attends this dream.

			You shall have friendship despite women who seek to harm you.

			You are warned of treachery in one near and dear to you.

			This denotes the fear of sickness and ill-health.

★	★		★	
★	★	★	★	
★	★		★	
★	★	★	★	
	★		★	★

You will suffer financial loss.

	★	★	★
★	★	★	★
★	★	★	
★	★	★	★
★	★	★	

You will shortly meet one who will become a true friend.

★	★	★	
★	★	★	★
	★	★	★
★	★	★	★
	★	★	★

You will travel and change your residence.

★	★	★	
	★	★	
	★	★	★
	★	★	
★	★	★	

Letters and news of absent friends.

	★	★	★
	★	★	
★	★	★	
	★	★	
	★	★	★

You have a powerful enemy who will seek to ruin you.

	★	★	★
	★	★	
	★	★	★
	★	★	
★	★	★	

A sad dream foretelling sickness and trouble.

★	★	★	
	★	★	
★	★	★	
	★	★	
	★	★	★

Annoyances will precede the rescue from your troubles.

★	★	★	
	★	★	
	★	★	★
	★	★	
	★	★	★

You will soon receive a sum of money.

★ ★ ★ Although a pleasant dream, it is
★ ★ unfortunate in meaning.
★ ★ ★
★ ★
★ ★ ★

★ ★ ★ Several translations fit this dream; a loss
★ ★ ★ ★ by theft, a gift and a funeral.
★ ★ ★
★ ★
★ ★ ★

★ ★ ★ Unfortunate for purse, person and
★ ★ ★ ★ property.
★ ★ ★
★ ★
★ ★ ★

★ ★ ★ On Monday and Wednesday, trouble;
★ ★ otherwise, news.
★ ★ ★
★ ★ ★ ★
★ ★ ★

★ ★ ★ News of absent friends.
★ ★
★ ★ ★
★ ★ ★ ★
★ ★ ★

★ ★ ★ A warning that you are in peril.
★ ★
★ ★ ★
★ ★ ★ ★
★ ★ ★

★ ★ ★ Danger from animals.
★ ★
★ ★ ★
★ ★ ★ ★
★ ★ ★

★ ★ ★ The scattering of your goods.
★ ★ ★ ★
★ ★ ★
★ ★
★ ★ ★

231

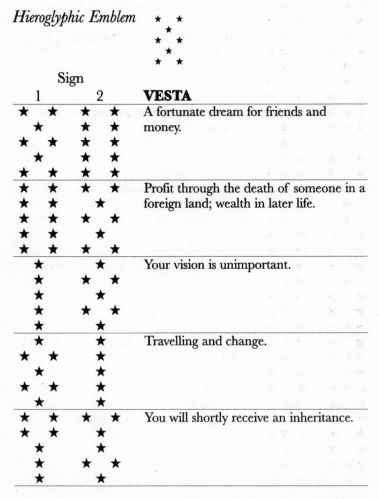

| | | | | Poverty in youth; riches in old age. |

Hieroglyphic Emblem

	Sign			
1		2		**VESTA**
				A fortunate dream for friends and money.
				Profit through the death of someone in a foreign land; wealth in later life.
				Your vision is unimportant.
				Travelling and change.
				You will shortly receive an inheritance.

★	★	★	★	A run of good fortune lies ahead.
	★		★ ★	
	★		★	
★	★		★	
	★		★	

	★		★	Feasting and joy: a wedding.
	★		★ ★	
	★		★	
★	★		★	
★	★	★	★	

	★		★	Wine, mirth, feasting; a marriage amongst your kin.
★	★		★	
	★		★	
	★	★	★	
★	★	★	★	

★	★	★	★	Evil news concerning friends.
★	★		★	
	★		★	
★	★		★	
★	★	★	★	

★	★	★	★	Letters and papers; also a secret foe.
	★		★ ★	
	★		★	
	★		★ ★	
★	★	★	★	

★	★	★	★	Danger of accidents near your home.
	★		★ ★	
★	★	★	★	
★	★		★	
★	★	★	★	

★	★	★	★	Watch your employees, lest they defraud you.
★	★		★	
★	★	★	★	
	★		★ ★	
★	★	★	★	

★	★	★	★	Trouble, harassments, cares.
★	★		★	
★	★	★	★	
★	★		★	
	★		★	

Unexpected riches from diverse sources.

This dream forewarns the dreamer of many malicious and treacherous foes.

Good by means of apparent evil and misfortune.

Trouble amongst your friends is here denoted; some are imprisoned, others will die.

Anger and contention are here forecast.

Marriage for a single man; to a married man, widowhood; to a female, courtship, love, friendship.

The dreamer is warned against poisonous liquids.

Crosses and griefs are here ominous.

A dream due to physical ailments.

Advancement, pride and ambition.

Good will come through religious friends.

A dream indicating unfulfilled desires.

Trouble, care, bereavement, even death are here foretold.

Before long you will be delivered from the peril into which you are prone to fall.

A joyous dream denoting deliverance from all your afflictions.

Many unfaithful friends to whom you have been faithful.

Danger to the dreamer from the falling of weights.

Many enemies against whom you shall prevail.

A long life but heavy sorrows.

Hieroglyphic Emblem

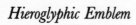

Sign

1	2	**PISCES**

Disappointment at home and in your business.

Many changes; travelling.

A friend will soon visit you.

236

```
★    ★        ★
   ★          ★
★    ★        ★
   ★          ★
   ★          ★
```
The handling of large sums of gold and silver.

```
★    ★        ★
★    ★     ★    ★
   ★       ★    ★
   ★          ★
   ★          ★
```
Scenes of grief and sorrow, also financial worries.

```
   ★       ★    ★
★    ★     ★    ★
★    ★        ★
   ★          ★
   ★          ★
```
Beware of fraud and cheats.

```
   ★       ★    ★
   ★          ★
   ★       ★    ★
★    ★     ★    ★
★    ★     ★    ★
```
Loss through theft or fraud.

```
★    ★        ★
   ★          ★
★    ★        ★
★    ★     ★    ★
★    ★     ★    ★
```
Strange, unexpected news.

```
★    ★        ★
★    ★     ★    ★
   ★       ★    ★
★    ★     ★    ★
★    ★     ★    ★
```
Social pleasures, new faces.

```
   ★       ★    ★
★    ★     ★    ★
★    ★        ★
★    ★     ★    ★
★    ★     ★    ★
```
A vain unprofitable vision.

```
★    ★        ★
★    ★     ★    ★
★    ★        ★
   ★          ★
★    ★     ★    ★
```
Danger of accidents and falls.

Avoid travel for a month after this dream. Danger.

To a female, love and courtship; to a male, rivals.

On the 11th day of the moon, vexations; on other days, removals.

Worrying letters or news.

Death will visit your family.

Festivities and social pleasures.

A wedding amongst your kindred.

Changes that will cause your business to flourish.

A large sum of money will shortly be yours.

Strife, quarrelling, fear of bloodshed.

Deceit and vanity.

A death among your family within a year.

Danger of fire is here forecast.

Letters and news.

Your troubles are nearly over.

Strangers are about to visit the dreamer.

★ ★ ★	Riding on horseback or travelling.

Riding on horseback or travelling.

False friends will seek to harm you.

Joy, love, prosperity are here indicated.

On the 3rd or 7th days of the moon this dream augurs sickness; on other days, grievances.

Vexation, grief and trouble.

Hieroglyphic Emblem

Sign		
1	2	**DIANA**

The advent of good fortune is predicted.

★ ★ ★ ★ Fortunate signs indicating business
★ ★ ★ ★ activity.
★ ★　★
★ ★ ★ ★
★ ★　★

　★　★ The revelation of secrets is here
　★　★ prophesied.
　★ ★ ★
　★　★
　★ ★ ★

　★　★ Danger from water is threatened.
　★　★
★ ★　★
　★　★
★ ★　★

★ ★ ★ ★ Approaching prosperity is here heralded.
★ ★ ★ ★
　★ ★ ★
　★　★
　★ ★ ★

★ ★ ★ ★ You shall have money.
★ ★ ★ ★
★ ★　★
　★　★
★ ★　★

　★　★ Diverse strange events are here denoted.
　★　★
　★ ★ ★
★ ★ ★ ★
★ ★　★

　★　★ Sorrow, care and loss.
　★　★
★ ★　★
★ ★ ★ ★
　★ ★ ★

★ ★ ★ ★ A false friend will cause you trouble.
★ ★ ★ ★
　★ ★ ★
★ ★ ★ ★
★ ★　★

★ ★ ★ ★				Sickness and ill-health to yourself and your family.
★ ★ ★ ★				
★ ★ · ★				
★ ★ ★ ★				
· ★ ★ ★				

★ ★ ★ ★				Treacherous enemies are endeavouring to harm you.
· ★ · ★				
★ ★ ★ ·				
★ ★ ★ ★				
★ ★ ★ ·				

★ ★ ★ ★				Beware signing documents.
· ★ · ★				
· ★ ★ ★				
★ ★ ★ ★				
· ★ ★ ★				

· ★ · ★				Pleasure and profit are here denoted.
★ ★ ★ ★				
★ ★ ★ ·				
★ ★ ★ ★				
★ ★ ★ ·				

· ★ · ★				You will soon receive good news.
★ ★ ★ ★				
· ★ ★ ★				
★ ★ ★ ★				
· ★ ★ ★				

· ★ · ★				On the moon's increase this dream foretells disaster; on the wane, funerals.
★ ★ ★ ★				
★ ★ · ★				
★ ★ ★ ★				
· ★ ★ ★				

· ★ · ★				Evil news is here predicted.
★ ★ ★ ★				
· ★ ★ ★				
★ ★ ★ ★				
★ ★ · ★				

★ ★ ★ ★				Long life and riches are here foretold.
· ★ · ★				
· ★ ★ ★				
· ★ · ★				
★ ★ · ★				

★ ★ ★ ★	A happy dream.
★ ★	
★ ★ ★	
★ ★	
★ ★ ★	

★ ★ ★ ★
 ★ ★
★ ★ ★ ★
 ★ ★ ★
 ★ ★
 ★ ★ ★

A happy dream.

★ ★
★ ★ ★ ★
 ★ ★ ★
 ★ ★
 ★ ★ ★

To the single this dream augurs marriage; to the wedded an increase of family.

★ ★
★ ★ ★ ★
★ ★ ★
 ★ ★
★ ★ ★

A dream of tears.

★ ★
★ ★
★ ★ ★
★ ★ ★ ★
★ ★ ★

Anger and quarrelling.

★ ★
★ ★
★ ★ ★
★ ★ ★ ★
★ ★ ★

A doubtful dream. Have a care.

★ ★
★ ★
★ ★ ★
★ ★
★ ★ ★

Your dream arises from physical disorder.

★ ★
★ ★
★ ★ ★
★ ★
★ ★ ★

A vision of clouds and shadows.

★ ★ ★ ★
★ ★
★ ★ ★
★ ★
★ ★ ★

Amity, joy, love.

```
★  ★   ★  ★     You will acquire money.
   ★      ★
★  ★      ★
   ★      ★
★  ★      ★
```

```
★  ★   ★  ★     Affliction and misfortune are here
★  ★   ★  ★     denoted.
★  ★      ★
   ★      ★
   ★   ★  ★
```

```
★  ★   ★  ★     Fortunate on the 1st, 5th and 11th days
★  ★   ★  ★     of the moon; on other days, evil.
   ★   ★  ★
   ★      ★
★  ★      ★
```

```
   ★      ★     Evil times follow this dream.
★  ★   ★  ★
★  ★      ★
   ★      ★
   ★   ★  ★
```

```
   ★      ★     Temptations to the female sex; to males
★  ★   ★  ★     pleasure.
   ★   ★  ★
   ★      ★
★  ★      ★
```

```
★  ★   ★  ★     You are warned that a deceitful friend is
   ★      ★     near you.
★  ★      ★
★  ★   ★  ★
   ★   ★  ★
```

```
★  ★   ★  ★     Anger concerning papers and books is
   ★      ★     here denoted.
   ★   ★  ★
★  ★   ★  ★
★  ★   ★
```

Hieroglyphic Emblem

```
★   ★
  ★
★   ★
★   ★
  ★
```

	Sign		
1		2	**MEDUSA**

Sign 1	Sign 2	Meaning

★ ★
  ★
★ ★
★ ★
  ★
	★ ★
	★ ★
	★ ★
	★ ★
	★ ★
		This warns the dreamer against a fair-haired attractive person.

★ ★
★ ★
★ ★
★ ★
★ ★
	★ ★
	  ★
	★ ★
	★ ★
	  ★
		Injury and misfortune to the rich; to the poor, comfort and help.

★ ★ ★ ★ ★	★ ★ ★ ★ ★ ★ ★	Shame or reproach; look to yourself.
★ ★ ★ ★ ★ ★ ★	★ ★ ★ ★ ★	Sickness threatens you.
★ ★ ★ ★ ★ ★ ★	★ ★ ★ ★ ★ ★ ★	Care to the rich; wealth to the poor.
★ ★ ★ ★ ★ ★ ★	★ ★ ★ ★ ★ ★ ★	Amorous friendships are here betokened.
★ ★ ★ ★ ★ ★ ★	★ ★ ★ ★ ★ ★ ★	Loss and treachery through servants.

245

A warning to beware of thieves.

On a Thursday this dream is an omen of many happy years to come; on other days, a good dream.

Strange news is on the way to you.

Accidents through weapons or four-footed animals.

Danger threatens the dreamer.

Sorrow and tears will soon come to you.

A promotion is here augured.

Trouble that will end in receipt of money.

★		★		Losses and damage are here signified.
★		★	★	
★	★	★	★	
★	★	★	★	
★		★	★	

★		★		Within three months after this dream
★	★	★		you will meet with some mishap.
★	★	★	★	
★	★	★	★	
★		★	★	

★		★		Very evil if dreamed on the 7th day of
★		★	★	the moon; it also denotes the paying out
★	★	★	★	of large sums of money.
★	★	★	★	
★	★	★		

★		★		You will attend both a wedding and a
★	★	★		funeral within a year.
★		★		
★		★		
★		★	★	

★		★		Let the dreamer beware of private
★		★	★	enemies.
★		★		
★		★		
★	★	★		

★		★		Deceitful pleasures are here foretold.
★		★	★	
★		★		
★	★	★	★	
★		★	★	

★		★		Travel and labour both in vain are here
★	★	★		signified.
★		★		
★	★	★	★	
★	★	★		

★	★	★	★	Many annoyances from enemies, but
★		★	★	eventual victory is here forecast.
★		★		
★		★		
★		★	★	

★	★	★	★	On Tuesday this dream denotes money;
★	★		★	on Wednesday or Friday, gifts; Monday, a
	★		★	friend; Thursday a ring; Saturday, a foe;
	★		★	Sunday a journey.
★	★		★	

★	★	★	★	Your dream predicts money.
★	★		★	
★	★	★	★	
	★		★	
	★		★	★

★	★	★	★	Good and lasting fortune.
	★		★	★
★	★	★	★	
	★		★	
★	★		★	

	★		★	Guard your purse.
★	★		★	
★	★	★	★	
	★		★	
	★	★	★	

	★		★	Sore affliction.
	★	★	★	
★	★	★	★	
	★		★	
★	★		★	

★	★	★	★	No good can come of this dream.
★	★		★	
	★		★	
★	★	★	★	
	★	★	★	

★	★	★	★	Hindrances in your affairs.
	★	★	★	
	★		★	
★	★	★	★	
★	★		★	

	★		★	Grief, heaviness, sorrow.
★	★		★	
★	★	★	★	
	★		★	
★	★		★	

★		★	
★	★	★	
★ ★	★	★	
★		★	
★		★	★

Sudden anger is here foretold.

Hieroglyphic Emblem

```
      ★
    ★ ★
    ★ ★
      ★
    ★ ★
```

Sign

1	2	**PHOEBUS**

★		★	★	Sadness, care, grief are here signified.
★	★	★	★	
★	★	★	★	
★		★	★	
★	★	★	★	

★	★	★		Dangers threaten you from a watery
★	★	★	★	element.
★	★	★	★	
★	★	★		
★	★	★	★	

★		★	★	Loss through theft or a secret foe.
★		★		
★		★		
★		★	★	
★		★		

★	★	★		You will receive joyful news.
★		★		
★		★		
★	★	★		
★		★		

★	★	★		Marriage to virgins and widows; to
★	★	★	★	others, riches.
★		★		
★		★	★	
★		★		

★		★	★	Health and vigour to the sick; to others an insignificant dream.
★	★	★	★	
	★		★	
★	★		★	
	★		★	

★		★	★	Business activity, profit.
★			★	
★			★	
★	★		★	
★	★	★	★	

★	★		★	Deliverance from your troubles is forecast.
	★		★	
	★		★	
	★		★	★
★	★		★	★

★	★		★	To a single person, marriage if dreamt on Wednesday; on Sunday, profit; on other days, good friends.
★	★		★	★
	★			★
★	★		★	
★	★		★	★

	★		★	★	A reward will come to you.
★	★		★	★
	★			★
	★		★	★
★	★		★	★

★	★			★	To the rich, secret envy; to the poor, assistance.
	★			★
★	★		★	★
★	★		★	
★	★		★	★

	★		★	★	Grief and danger will beset the dreamer.
	★		★	
★	★		★	★
	★		★	★
★	★		★	★

★	★			★	On the 13th day of the moon, death; on other days, sickness.
★	★		★	★
★	★		★	★
	★		★	★
★	★		★	★

Your undertakings will prosper after this dream.

You will discover some hidden secrets.

Your adversaries and foes will meet with ruin after this dream.

Riches and honour will follow this dream.

You will be invited to celebrations after this dream.

Death is about to deprive you of an enemy.

The dreamer will be invited to a wedding.

You are warned of spiteful enemies.

A funeral among your relatives is approaching.

You will make new friends, but you are warned not to trust them.

You will shortly receive money.

Attainment of wishes is here denoted.

Deliverance from loss or hurt, which heretofore overhung the dreamer.

Sadness, or sad news is here prognosticated.

An obstruction in your business is here denoted.

This dream on a Sunday foretells love; Monday, sickness; Wednesday, a gift; Friday, friendship; other days, losses.

★ ★ ★ ★ ★ ★ ★ ★ ★ ★ ★ ★ ★ ★ ★ ★	Be careful of writing letters; trouble thereby is signified.
★ ★ ★ ★ ★ ★ ★ ★ ★ ★ ★ ★ ★ ★	Enemies are trying to bar your path. Beware.
★ ★ ★ ★ ★ ★ ★ ★ ★ ★ ★ ★ ★ ★	A tall, fair man shall prove an adversary.

Hieroglyphic Emblem

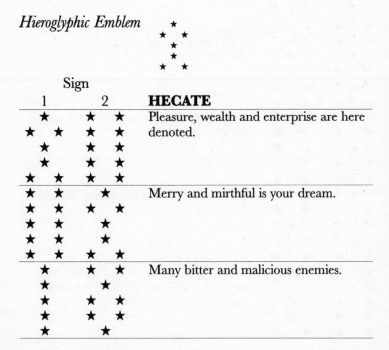

Sign			
1		2	**HECATE**
★ ★ ★ ★ ★ ★ ★ ★ ★ ★ ★ ★ ★ ★ ★ ★ ★			Pleasure, wealth and enterprise are here denoted.
★ ★ ★ ★ ★ ★ ★ ★ ★ ★ ★ ★ ★ ★ ★ ★ ★			Merry and mirthful is your dream.
★ ★ ★ ★ ★ ★ ★ ★ ★ ★ ★ ★ ★			Many bitter and malicious enemies.

253

You will have the help of a rich friend.

Delay, obstacles and inactivity.

You will receive money.

Success and profit.

Evil news is on the way to you.

There is slander about you; be on your guard.

Unlucky on all days except the 3rd of the moon.

On Tuesday this dream shows an enemy; Monday, a false friend; other days it is unimportant.

★	★	★	Pleasure and social gatherings.

Pleasure and social gatherings.

Merry-makings that will end in sorrow are at hand.

Weddings to which the dreamer will be invited.

Before long you will lose a respected friend through death.

A joyous dream.

Feasting and mirth are here indicated.

Success in your pursuits.

You will move from your residence.

Hasty and extraordinary news is at hand.

Profit and enterprise.

You will make a new and profitable friend.

A fortunate dream.

Sickness is at hand.

On Friday, disaster; on other days, tears.

To a man this dream is a warning to beware of pleasure; to a female it warns that one is near who seeks her disgrace.

Delay in your wishes and their fulfilment.

★ ★ ★				Letters and news are here prognosticated.
★ ★ ★ ★				
★ ★ ★				
★ ★ ★				
★ ★				

A spiteful and malicious person envies the dreamer.

Death and funerals among your relatives.

Before long you will take a journey.

The dreamer is warned to act discreetly as he is watched.

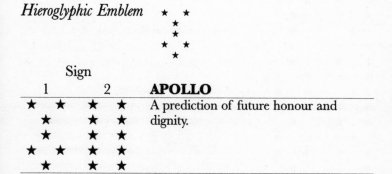

Hieroglyphic Emblem

Sign
1   2   **APOLLO**

A prediction of future honour and dignity.

257

★	★	★	★	The dreamer will receive a gift of money.
★	★	★		
★	★	★		
★	★	★	★	
★	★	★		

	★		★	Troubles are upon the dreamer.
	★	★	★	
	★	★	★	
	★	★		
	★	★	★	

	★		★	Happiness and wealth.
★	★		★	
★	★		★	
	★		★	
★	★		★	

★	★	★	★	Health, wealth and friends.
★	★		★	
	★	★	★	
	★		★	
	★	★	★	

★	★	★	★	Enterprise and profit are here
	★	★	★	predicted.
★	★		★	
	★		★	
★	★		★	

	★		★	Evil is near at hand.
	★	★	★	
	★	★	★	
★	★	★	★	
★	★	★		

	★		★	A dream that heralds sorrow.
★	★	★		
★	★	★		
★	★	★	★	
	★	★	★	

★	★	★	★	Malice and strife of enemies.
★	★		★	
	★	★	★	
★	★	★	★	
★	★		★	

★ ★ ★ ★ ★ ★ ★ ★ ★ ★ ★ ★ ★ ★ ★ ★ ★				Treachery from which you shall escape.

★ ★ ★ ★ ★ ★ ★ ★ ★ ★ ★ ★ ★ ★ ★ ★ ★				Trouble is at hand.

★ ★ ★ ★ ★ ★ ★ ★ ★ ★ ★ ★ ★ ★ ★ ★ ★				On a Sunday your dream is evil; Monday it brings news; Tuesday, treachery; Wednesday, letters; other days, anger.

★ ★ ★ ★ ★ ★ ★ ★ ★ ★ ★ ★ ★ ★ ★				Years of wealth and happiness are predicted here.

★ ★ ★ ★ ★ ★ ★ ★ ★ ★ ★ ★ ★ ★ ★				Quarrels, rivals in love.

★ ★ ★ ★ ★ ★ ★ ★ ★ ★ ★ ★ ★ ★ ★ ★ ★ ★				One of your family will soon die.

★ ★ ★ ★ ★ ★ ★ ★ ★ ★ ★ ★ ★ ★ ★ ★ ★ ★				Great adversaries and many of them.

★ ★ ★ ★ ★ ★ ★ ★ ★ ★ ★ ★ ★ ★ ★				Wealth and poverty are here predicted.

★　　　　★ ★　　★　★ ★　　★　★ ★　★　★　★ ★　　★　★	Quarrels over money.
★　★　★　★ ★　　★　★ ★　　★　★ ★　　★ ★　★　★	Promotion in your business or everyday life.
★　★　★　★ ★　★　★ ★　★　★ ★　　★ ★　★　★	Evil news is at hand although no harm will come of it.
★　　　★ ★　★　★ ★　　★　★ ★　　★ ★　★　★	This dream is an omen of a funeral.
★　　　★ ★　★　★ ★　★　★ ★　　★ ★　★　★	Sickness is hereby foretold.
★　　　★ ★　★　★ ★　★　★ ★　　★ ★　★　★	If dreamt on the 3rd, 5th, 7th or 10th days, death within a year.
★　　　★ ★　★　★ ★　★　★ ★　　★ ★　★　★	A dream arising from anxiety. It is not prophetic.
★　　　★ ★　★　★ ★　★　★ ★　★　★ ★　★　★	Evil is here prophesied to the dreamer.

Beware of secret enemies.

On Sunday this dream predicts a present; on Thursday a loss through a bad debt; insignificant otherwise.

A prediction of many troubles.

A good dream, promising money.

Profitless pleasures are here denoted.

You will soon meet with kind friends.

Pleasures, new scenes, happiness.

Hieroglyphic Emblem

Sign 1		Sign 2		FORTUNA
★	★	★	★	Ominous; a funeral among your relatives
★	★	★	★	within the year.
	★	★	★	
	★	★	★	
★	★	★	★	
★	★	★	★	Secret cares and grief.
★	★	★	★	
★	★	★		
★	★	★		
★	★	★	★	
	★		★	Misfortunes for a season.
	★		★	
	★	★	★	
	★	★	★	
	★		★	
	★		★	On Saturday, accident; on other days
	★		★	trouble.
★	★		★	
★	★		★	
	★		★	
★	★	★	★	The approach of a beneficial, prosperous
★	★	★	★	influence.
	★	★	★	
	★	★	★	
	★		★	
★	★	★	★	After expenditures money will come.
★	★	★	★	
★	★	★		
★	★	★		
	★	★		
	★		★	You are warned against misplaced trust.
	★		★	
	★	★	★	
★	★	★		
★	★	★	★	

To a male this dream augurs trouble through one of the opposite sex.

Strange news approaches the dreamer.

Enterprise and business activity.

Beware of a false friend.

A warning not to lend money, in case you are cheated.

The approach of something joyful and good.

Pleasure and mirth.

This dream informs you of the illness of an absent friend.

★ ★ ★ ★ ★ ★ ★ ★ ★ ★ ★ ★ ★ ★	Guard your speech; speak against no one.
★ ★ ★ ★ ★ ★ ★ ★ ★ ★ ★ ★	Anger will cause you trouble.
★ ★ ★ ★ ★ ★ ★ ★ ★ ★ ★ ★	A change of residence is here forecast.
★ ★ ★ ★ ★ ★ ★ ★ ★ ★ ★ ★ ★ ★	To the sick, peril; to the well, disappointment.
★ ★ ★ ★ ★ ★ ★ ★ ★ ★ ★ ★ ★ ★	Beware of secret foes.
★ ★ ★ ★ ★ ★ ★ ★ ★ ★ ★ ★ ★ ★	You are warned of an unpleasant occurrence about your person or in your home.
★ ★ ★ ★ ★ ★ ★ ★ ★ ★ ★ ★ ★ ★	Watch for a concealed enemy near at hand.
★ ★ ★ ★ ★ ★ ★ ★ ★ ★ ★ ★ ★ ★	On Sunday, good news; Monday, a quarrel; other days, money.

		Great prosperity is here foretold.

		You will see someone who is trying to help you.

		A marriage is here forecast.

		You shall attain your wishes.

		Money and friends are foretold.

		Delays followed by a month of prosperity.

		Danger from injury by animals.

		Your wishes will be delayed in fulfilment.

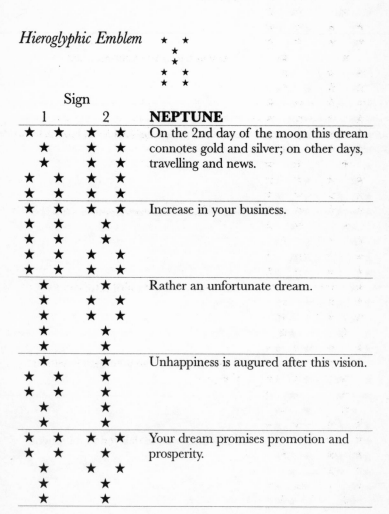

				An unfortunate dream in diverse ways.

Hieroglyphic Emblem

	Sign			
1		2		**NEPTUNE**

On the 2nd day of the moon this dream connotes gold and silver; on other days, travelling and news.

Increase in your business.

Rather an unfortunate dream.

Unhappiness is augured after this vision.

Your dream promises promotion and prosperity.

You shall receive wealth and power.

Prosperity to a man; to a woman, marriage.

You will overcome your enemies.

Annoyances and insults from enemies.

Avoid litigation, warns your dream self.

See to your health, illness is foretold.

Trouble; a death in your family within the year.

Evil tidings are here forecast.

★   ★   ★   ★
    ★   ★   ★
    ★   ★   ★
 ★   ★   ★   ★
    ★   ★
	Success and comfort for the remainder of your life.

★ ★ ★ ★ ★ ★ ★ ★ ★ ★ ★ ★ ★ ★	To the sick this dream denotes speedy recovery.

★   ★
    ★   ★   ★
    ★   ★   ★
 ★   ★   ★   ★
    ★   ★
	You are warned not to undertake important business on the day succeeding this dream.

★   ★
 ★   ★   ★
    ★   ★   ★
    ★   ★
    ★   ★
	To a male this dream denotes a happy union with his beloved.

★   ★
    ★   ★   ★
 ★   ★   ★
    ★   ★
    ★   ★
	Celebrations; an especially pleasant invitation.

★   ★
    ★   ★   ★
    ★   ★   ★
    ★   ★
 ★   ★   ★   ★
	Many troubles and cares will follow this dream.

★ ★ ★ ★ ★ ★ ★ ★ ★ ★ ★ ★ ★ ★	Enemies will harm you; be on your guard.

★   ★   ★   ★
    ★   ★   ★
    ★   ★   ★
    ★   ★
    ★   ★
	On Wednesday, Thursday or Friday, the acquisition of riches; on other days, friends.

★ ★ ★ ★   A fortunate, prosperous dream.
★ ★ ★
★ ★ ★
 ★ ★
 ★ ★

 ★ ★   Prosperous enterprises.
 ★ ★ ★
★ ★ ★
★ ★ ★ ★
★ ★ ★ ★

 ★ ★   Good news is at hand.
★ ★ ★
 ★ ★ ★
★ ★ ★ ★
★ ★ ★ ★

 ★ ★   Improvement in financial conditions and
 ★ ★ ★ peace of mind.
★ ★ ★
★ ★ ★
 ★ ★

 ★ ★   Pain, and sorrow, and toil.
★ ★ ★
 ★ ★ ★
 ★ ★ ★
 ★ ★

★ ★ ★ ★   Enemies are working for your undoing;
 ★ ★ ★ have a care.
★ ★ ★
 ★ ★ ★
★ ★ ★ ★

★ ★ ★ ★   Money is here foretold.
★ ★ ★
 ★ ★ ★
★ ★ ★
★ ★ ★ ★

 ★ ★   A visit from absent ones from afar.
★ ★ ★
 ★ ★ ★
 ★ ★
★ ★ ★ ★

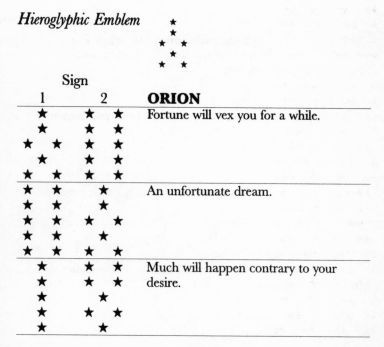

Trouble among your family.

A marriage is near.

One whom you have thought a friend will become an enemy.

Hieroglyphic Emblem

Sign

1   2   **ORION**

Fortune will vex you for a while.

An unfortunate dream.

Much will happen contrary to your desire.

```
★   ★      ★        A friend will deliver you from some
★   ★      ★        heavy trouble.
    ★      ★
★   ★      ★
    ★      ★
```

```
★   ★      ★        Benefits from a great personage.
★   ★      ★
    ★      ★
    ★          ★   ★
    ★          ★
```

```
    ★      ★   ★     Injury from an animal, or a fall
    ★      ★   ★     is predicted.
    ★      ★
★   ★      ★
    ★      ★
```

```
    ★      ★   ★     See to your health; sickness threatens.
    ★      ★   ★
    ★      ★
★   ★   ★   ★
★   ★   ★   ★
```

```
★   ★      ★        On Sunday, Tuesday or Thursday,
★   ★      ★        honour and friends; on other days,
    ★      ★        friends.
★   ★   ★   ★
★   ★   ★   ★
```

```
★   ★      ★        Persecution from contemptible persons.
★   ★      ★
    ★      ★
★   ★      ★
★   ★   ★   ★
```

```
    ★      ★   ★     Loss of credit and of friends.
    ★      ★   ★
    ★      ★
    ★      ★   ★
★   ★   ★   ★
```

```
★   ★      ★        A sorrowful dream.
    ★      ★   ★
★   ★   ★   ★
★   ★   ★
★   ★   ★   ★
```

You are warned against excess.

Good fortune and prosperity are foretold.

Anger and strife are predicted.

A fortunate dream indicating wealth and health.

Wealth in due course.

A change for the worse in your fortunes.

A legacy will be yours shortly.

A dream of illusions, broken promises.

Guard your speech and action; treacherous friends surround you.

Travel in strange lands.

Money through wit and wisdom.

Saturday this dream brings a rich gift; Sunday, a journey; Wednesday, labour in vain; other days, profit.

On the increase of the moon, weddings, festivals.

News and various gossip and reports.

Avoid quarrels if you wish to escape sorrow.

A sharp tongue will slander or trouble you.

273

★ ★	★		Strife and discord.
★	★ ★		
★ ★	★ ★		
★ ★	★		
★	★		

★	★ ★		You are warned of misfortune and loss
★ ★	★		of money.
★	★		
★	★ ★		
★ ★	★ ★		

★ ★	★		Although many of the sorrows are over,
★	★ ★		be cautious.
★	★		
★ ★	★		
★ ★	★ ★		

Hieroglyphic Emblem

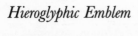

Sign

1	2	**FINIS**
★	★ ★	Beware a quarrelsome person who is
★	★ ★	near you.
★ ★	★ ★	
★	★ ★	
★	★ ★	

1	2	
★ ★	★	Eschew strife, angry words and
★ ★	★	contention.
★ ★	★ ★	
★ ★	★	
★ ★	★	

1	2	
★	★ ★	If your dream pertains to business it
★	★ ★	denotes enterprise and activity.
★	★	
★	★ ★	
★	★ ★	

★ ★ ★ ★ ★ ★ ★ ★ ★ ★ ★ ★ ★ ★	Changes and removals.
★ ★ ★ ★ ★ ★ ★ ★ ★ ★ ★ ★ ★ ★	You will finally succeed.
★ ★ ★ ★ ★ ★ ★ ★ ★ ★ ★ ★ ★ ★	A dream of financial success.
★ ★ ★ ★ ★ ★ ★ ★ ★ ★ ★ ★ ★ ★	You are in danger of being wronged by friends and neighbours.
★ ★ ★ ★ ★ ★ ★ ★ ★ ★ ★ ★ ★ ★	Business enterprise.
★ ★ ★ ★ ★ ★ ★ ★ ★ ★ ★ ★ ★ ★ ★ ★	Take heed lest flatterers mislead you.
★ ★ ★ ★ ★ ★ ★ ★ ★ ★ ★ ★ ★ ★ ★ ★	Labour, strife and sorrow are here forecast.
★ ★ ★ ★ ★ ★ ★ ★ ★ ★ ★ ★ ★ ★ ★ ★	The dream shows an uneasy mind.

275

A powerful friend shall cross your path.

Marriage, but be not hasty.

A vain person is jealous of you.

Riches in old age.

You have enemies but they can do no harm.

Beware of back-biters and false friends.

You shall triumph over subtle enemies.

Beware of water after this dream.

A funeral approaches the dreamer.

Changes and troubles are here manifest.

One whom you have befriended will vex and annoy you.

Many secret enemies.

Victory over enemies if dreamed on Tuesday; otherwise, ill.

Many and varied misfortunes assail the dreamer.

Perils, though they are passing.

Fortune and success.

				An offer of matrimony to the single.

★		★	★	An offer of matrimony to the single.
★	★	★		
	★	★		
★	★	★		
★	★	★		
★	★	★		To a female, disappointed love.
★	★	★		
★	★	★	★	
	★	★	★	
	★	★	★	
★		★	★	Although your dream was tempestuous it bodes no harm.
	★	★	★	
★	★	★	★	
★	★	★		
★	★	★		
★	★		★	Do not place too much faith in friends.
	★	★	★	
★	★	★	★	
★	★	★		
	★	★	★	
★		★	★	On Tuesday or Saturday, quarrels; Friday, courtship; other days, unimportant.
★	★	★		
★	★	★	★	
	★	★	★	
★	★	★		

Appendix

Adler, Alfred (1870–1937) Austrian psychiatrist and an associate of FREUD, although he rejected Freud's emphasis on sexuality. He founded a school of psychoanalysis based on the individual's quest to overcome feelings of inadequacy (the 'inferiority complex'). His main works were *The Practice and Theory of Individual Psychology* (1923), and *Understanding Human Nature* (1927).

Artemidorus Daldianus (c. 120 AD) compiler of a five-volume dream book, *Oneirocritica*, which some say forms the basis of the mystical side of dream interpretation today. He differentiates between the dreams of kings and commoners, and universal and individual interpretation. Dreams which represent something as happening to the individual who dreams them, show that they have a personal significance. If the dream relates to another it will concern him alone.

Ellis, Henry Havelock (1859–1939) English physician and writer on the psychology of sex. He wrote *Studies in the Psychology of Sex* (1897–1928), the first objective study of the subject of sexual capacity which caused great controversy at the time.

Freud, Sigmund (1856–1939) Austrian neurologist and founder of the psychoanalytic movement. He worked with Austrian neurologist Josef Breuer (1842–1925) in using hypnosis to find the cause of hysterical illness. His work with Jean Martin Charcot (1825–1893) led to the development of 'free association' instead of hypnosis and together they sought to perfect the psychoanalytic method.

Freud's revolutionary theories on psychosexual behaviour,

and in particular infantile sexuality, caused controversy and lost him many friends and colleagues. Despite this he published *Die Traumdeutung* (1900) (The Interpretation of Dreams). This developed his theory, that neuroses are caused by repressed sexual urges, to apply to the content of dreams. Dream symbols are the disguised representation of forbidden sexual desires.

Alfred ADLER and Carl JUNG were like-minded colleagues of Freud's, involved in the founding of the Psychoanalytical Association, but both broke with Freud to develop their own theories on psychoanalysis. Freud developed his psychosexual theory further to describe the structure of the subconscious mind into three parts: id, ego, and superego.

His work is viewed as flawed and restricting by modern psychologists, but Freud's contribution to psychoanalysis was revolutionary in that he made the establishment consider that there could be non-physiological explanations for disordered behaviour. He died of cancer in 1939.

geomancy divining by the earth; derived from two Greek words, Ge, the earth, and Manteai, prophesy. Practised by the Chinese, in the Sudan, Egypt and in India. Diviners drew magic figures upon the earth before inks and pens had come into general use.

Jung, Carl Gustav (1875–1961) Swiss psychiatrist and follower of FREUD until 1913 with the publication of his book *The Psychology of the Unconscious* where Jung proposed ideas that were radically different from Freud's. He started a school of analytical psychology that combined Freudianism with humanistic psychology. Jung regarded the libido as part of our general biological function. Jung also emphasized the importance of the 'collective unconscious' as well as the personal conscience that Freud stressed. He catalogued various personality types; the most important of which were the 'introvert' and 'extrovert' types. Jung also wrote at length on religious symbolism and the meaning of life.

Laing, Ronald David (1927–1989) Scottish existential psychiatrist, and writer of *The Divided Self* (1960). His ideas on the approach to mental health were revolutionary. Rather than trying to cure the patient of their symptoms Laing proposed that psychiatrist and patient should accept that having a mental illness, such as schizophrenia, is a unique and positive experience. His writing later led him into the field of existential philosophy and also poetry.

latent content the latent content of dreams is the presumed meaning behind the MANIFEST CONTENT.

manifest content the manifest content of the dream is the actual apparent content of the dream, which acts symbolically to represent the LATENT CONTENT.

oneirocriticism a term, now out of use, meaning the interpretation of dreams.

oneiromancy another archaism meaning divination by the content of dreams.

Raphael (*c.* 1800) an astrologer and oneiromantic of the nineteenth century who published a *Royal Book of Dreams*. This he claimed to have unearthed in the form of an ancient manuscript and in it he gives an explanation of GEOMANCY and the art of dream interpretation.

Dream Diary

Sometimes it is difficult to remember all the details of a dream. A useful aid in interpreting your dreams is a dream diary. Keep a pencil and paper next to your bed and when you wake from a dream, quickly note what you can remember of it. You need not try to recall every small detail of the dream, just record the strong images and sensations that come to you. Keeping concise notes about your dreams will help you to identify recurring themes and symbols that can be interpreted with the help of this book. Do not forget that some dream symbols will have a particular significance for you personally, with a unique interpretation referring to your own experience, and this reading should take priority in the analysis.

Date:

_____

Content of dream:

_____

_____

_____

_____

_____

_____

_____

_____

_____

Significant theme / s:

_____

_____

_____

Symbols:

_____

_____

_____

Emotions that were felt:

_____

_____

_____

_____

_____

Recent events in life:

_____
_____
_____
_____
_____

People who were dreamed about and possible significance:

_____
_____
_____
_____
_____
_____
_____

Personal interpretation:

_____
_____
_____
_____
_____
_____
_____
_____
_____
_____
_____
_____
_____
_____
_____
_____
_____

Date:
_____

Content of dream:
_____
_____
_____
_____
_____
_____
_____
_____
_____
_____

Significant theme/s:
_____
_____
_____
_____

Symbols:
_____
_____
_____
_____

Emotions that were felt:
_____
_____
_____
_____
_____

Recent events in life:

_____
_____
_____
_____
_____

People who were dreamed about and possible significance:

_____
_____
_____
_____
_____
_____
_____

Personal interpretation:

_____
_____
_____
_____
_____
_____
_____
_____
_____
_____
_____
_____
_____
_____
_____

Dictionary of Dreams